Solutions and Workbook

for
Mathematics for Business
*5th Edition**

Natalie Yang

*by Gary Bronson
Richard Bronson
Maureen Kieff
Natalie Yang

ACKNOWLEDGMENT

I would like to thank Dr. Gary Bronson, Dr. Richard Bronson, Professor Kieff and the MISDS Department Chair, Dr. Wang, for their support in this endeavor. I would also like to express my appreciation to my former student, Bruce Tirrell, for catching several errors in the previous version of this solution manual.

DEDICATION

To Hong, Rachel, Benjamin, and My Parents

NOTES

1. Excel is a registered trademark of Microsoft Corporation.

2. Every effort has been made to make this solution manual as accurate as possible. No warranty of suitability, purpose, or fitness is implied, and the information is provided on an as is basis. The author assumes no liability or responsibility to any person or entity with respect to loss or damage from the use of the information contained in this manual.

3. There may be a small discrepancy between the answers in this manual and the Excel spreadsheet output because the spreadsheet internal calculations use higher precision.

4. The **Workbook** is located on page 105.

Table of Contents

Chapter 1 The Basics: A Review

Section 1.1: Signed Numbers

1. $3 + (-6) = -3$

3. $19.7 + (-18.1) = 1.6$

5. $-9 + \left(-\frac{1}{2}\right) = -\left(9 + \frac{1}{2}\right) = -9\frac{1}{2} = -\frac{19}{2}$

7. $9(18) = 162$

9. $(-9)(18) = -(9 \cdot 18) = -162$

11. $(2)\left(-\frac{1}{3}\right) = -\left(2 \cdot \frac{1}{3}\right) = -\left(\frac{2}{1} \cdot \frac{1}{3}\right) = -\frac{2}{3}$

13. $(-6.1)(2.3) = -(6.1 \cdot 2.3) = -14.03$

15. $\frac{(-8)}{(-2)} = \frac{8}{2} = 4$

17. $\frac{-8}{2} = -\frac{8}{2} = -4$

19. $\frac{4}{-5} = -\frac{4}{5}$

21. $\frac{-22}{4} = -\frac{2 \cdot 11}{2 \cdot 2} = -\frac{11}{2} = -5.5$

23. $4 - 8 = 4 + (-8) = -4$

25. $-4 - (-8) = -4 + 8 = 4$

27. $-8 - (-4) = (-8) + 4 = -4$

29. $-5.6 - 2.1 = (-5.6) + (-2.1) = -7.7$

31. $2[5 + (-3)] = 2[2] = 2 \cdot 2 = 4$

33. $-4(1 - 3) + 2(2 - 5) = -4(-2) + 2(-3) = 8 + (-6) = 2$

35. $(1.6)(1.9 - 2.1) - 6.3 = (1.6)(-0.2) - 6.3 = -0.32 - 6.3 = (-0.32) + (-6.3) = -6.62$

37. $\frac{8[1-(-8)]-2[7-1]}{2} = \frac{8[1+8]-2[6]}{2} = \frac{8[9]-2[6]}{2} = \frac{8 \cdot 9 - 2 \cdot 6}{2} = \frac{72-12}{2} = \frac{60}{2} = 30$

39. $\frac{(5-11)(8-14)+42(2+3)}{7[2(1+30)-3(2-5)]} = \frac{(-6)(-6)+42(5)}{7[2(31)-3(-3)]} = \frac{36+210}{7[62+9]} = \frac{246}{7[71]} = \frac{246}{497}$

Section 1.2: Solving Equations Having One Unknown

1. $x = -1$ is a solution to $2x + 3 = 1$ if it satisfies the given equation. Substituting $x = -1$ into the equation, we have: $2(-1) + 3 = -2 + 3 = 1$. Since $x = -1$ satisfied the equation, it is a solution.

3. $p = 1$ is a solution to $2(p + 7) = 3p + 4$ if it satisfies the given equation. Substituting $p = 1$ into the equation, we have:

Left side of the equation: $2(1 + 7) = 2(8) = 16$

Right side of the equation: $3(1) + 4 = 3 + 4 = 7$

Since the left and right sides of the equation do not equal, $p = 1$ is not a solution.

5. $s = 1$ is a solution to $\dfrac{(s+3)(s-2)}{2s+1} = s + 7$ if it satisfies the given equation. Substituting $s = 1$ into the equation, we have:

Left side of the equation: $\dfrac{(s+3)(s-2)}{2s+1} = \dfrac{(1+3)(1-2)}{2(1)+1} = \dfrac{(4)(-1)}{2+1} = \dfrac{-4}{3} = -\dfrac{4}{3}$

Right side of the equation: $s + 7 = 1 + 7 = 8$

Since the left and right sides of the equation do not equal, $s = 1$ is not a solution.

7. $x = 1$ is a solution to $\dfrac{x(y-1)+yz}{y(x-z)} = \dfrac{x}{y}$ if it satisfies the given equation. Substituting $x = 1$ into the equation, we have:

Left side of the equation: $\dfrac{1(2-1)+2(0)}{2(1-0)} = \dfrac{1(1)+0}{2(1)} = \dfrac{1}{2}$

Right side of the equation: $\dfrac{x}{y} = \dfrac{1}{2}$.

Since the left and right sides of the equation are equal, $x = 1$ is a solution.

9. $\begin{aligned} 7 &= 2 + x \\ -2 &\quad -2 \\ 5 &= x \quad or \quad x = 5 \end{aligned}$

11. $\begin{aligned} 8x &= -16 \\ \dfrac{8x}{8} &= \dfrac{-16}{8} \\ x &= -2 \end{aligned}$

13. $\begin{aligned} -4p &= 16 \\ \dfrac{-4p}{-4} &= \dfrac{16}{-4} \\ p &= -4 \end{aligned}$

15. $\begin{aligned} t - 10 &= 4 - t \\ +t &\qquad\quad +t \\ 2t - 10 &= 4 \\ +10 &\quad +10 \\ 2t &= 14 \\ \dfrac{2t}{2} &= \dfrac{14}{2} \\ t &= 7 \end{aligned}$

17. $\begin{aligned} 2x &= 3(x + 1) \\ 2x &= 3x + 3 \\ -3x &\quad -3x \\ -1x &= 3 \\ \dfrac{-1x}{-1} &= \dfrac{3}{-1} \\ x &= -3 \end{aligned}$

19. $8(p - 2) = 7(2p + 1)$

$8p - 16 = 14p + 7$

$\underline{-14p - 14p}$

$-6p - 16 = 7$

$\underline{+16 +16}$

$-6p = 23$

$$\frac{-6p}{-6} = \frac{23}{-6}$$

$$p = -\frac{23}{6}$$

21. $2(a + 7) - 4 = 3(a - 1) + 2a$

$2a + 14 - 4 = 3a - 3 + 2a$

$2a + 10 = 5a - 3$

$\underline{-5a - 5a}$

$-3a + 10 = -3$

$\underline{-10 - 10}$

$-3a = -13$

$$\frac{-3a}{-3} = \frac{-13}{-3}$$

$$a = \frac{-13}{-3} = \frac{13}{3}$$

23. $\dfrac{2(y-1)+4}{y} = 8$

$y \cdot \left[\dfrac{2(y-1)+4}{y}\right] = 8 \cdot y$

$\cancel{y} \cdot \left[\dfrac{2(y-1)+4}{\cancel{y}}\right] == 8 \cdot y$

$2(y - 1) + 4 = 8y$

$2y - 2 + 4 = 8y$

$\underline{-2y - 2y}$

$2 = 6y$

$\dfrac{2}{6} = \dfrac{6y}{6}$ or $\dfrac{6y}{6} = \dfrac{2}{6}$

$y = \dfrac{2}{6} = \dfrac{1}{3}$

25. $\dfrac{3(2t-6)+4(t-8)}{7(6+t)-8(t-4)} = -3$

$\dfrac{6t-18+4t-32}{42+7t-8t+32} = -3$

$\dfrac{10t-50}{-t+74} = -3$

$(-t + 74) \cdot \left[\dfrac{10t-50}{-t+74}\right] = -3 \cdot (-t + 74)$

$\cancel{(-t + 74)} \cdot \left[\dfrac{10t-50}{\cancel{-t+74}}\right] = -3 \cdot (-t + 74)$

$10t - 50 = 3t - 222$

$\underline{-3t - 3t}$

$7t - 50 = -222$

$\underline{+50 + 50}$

$7t = -172$

$\dfrac{7t}{7} = \dfrac{-172}{7}$

$t = -\dfrac{172}{7}$

Section 1.3: Exponents

1. $\dfrac{3^5 3^4}{3^2 3^3} = \dfrac{3^{5+4}}{3^{2+3}} = \dfrac{3^9}{3^5} = 3^{9-5} = 3^4 = 81$

3. $\dfrac{\pi^4 \left(\pi^2\right)^3}{\left(\pi^{-2}\right)^4 \pi^3} = \dfrac{\pi^4 \pi^6}{\pi^{-8} \pi^3} = \dfrac{\pi^{4+6}}{\pi^{-8+3}} = \dfrac{\pi^{10}}{\pi^{-5}} = \pi^{10-(-5)} = \pi^{10+5} = \pi^{15}$

5. $\dfrac{(1.7)^{8.1}(1.7)^{-3.4}}{(1.7)^{-4.1}(1.7)^{3.7}} = \dfrac{(1.7)^{8.1+(-3.4)}}{(1.7)^{-4.1+3.7}} = \dfrac{(1.7)^{4.7}}{(1.7)^{-0.4}} = (1.7)^{4.7-(-0.4)} = (1.7)^{4.7+0.4} = (1.7)^{5.1}$

7. $\dfrac{\left(y^{-3}\right)^{-2} y^4 y^{-1}}{y^2 \left(y^3\right)^{-1}} = \dfrac{y^6 y^4 y^{-1}}{y^2 y^{-3}} = \dfrac{y^{6+4+(-1)}}{y^{2+(-3)}} = \dfrac{y^9}{y^{-1}} = y^{9-(-1)} = y^{9+1} = y^{10}$

9. $\left\{\left[(3.1)^{-2}\right]^{-4}\right\}^3 = \left\{\left[(3.1)^{(-2)(-4)}\right]\right\}^3 = \left\{\left[(3.1)^8\right]\right\}^3 = (3.1)^{8(3)} = (3.1)^{24}$

11. $16^{-5/4} = \left(2^4\right)^{-\frac{5}{4}} = 2^{4\left(-\frac{5}{4}\right)} = 2^{-\frac{20}{4}} = 2^{-5} = \dfrac{1}{2^5} = \dfrac{1}{32}$

13. $100^{-3/2} = \left(10^2\right)^{-\frac{3}{2}} = 10^{2\left(-\frac{3}{2}\right)} = 10^{-\frac{6}{2}} = 10^{-3} = \dfrac{1}{10^3} = \dfrac{1}{1000}$

15. $\left(3^{1/3}\right)\left(9^{1/3}\right) = 3^{\frac{1}{3}}\left(3^2\right)^{\frac{1}{3}} = 3^{\frac{1}{3}} \, 3^{2 \cdot \frac{1}{3}} = 3^{\frac{1}{3}} \, 3^{\frac{2}{3}} = 3^{\frac{1}{3}+\frac{2}{3}} = 3^{\frac{3}{3}} = 3^1 = 3$

17. $\left(2^{-3/2}\right)\left(32^{-3/2}\right) = 2^{-\frac{3}{2}}\left(2^5\right)^{-\frac{3}{2}} = 2^{-\frac{3}{2}} \, 2^{5\left(-\frac{3}{2}\right)} = 2^{-\frac{3}{2}} \, 2^{-\frac{15}{2}} = 2^{-\frac{3}{2}+\left(-\frac{15}{2}\right)} = 2^{-\frac{18}{2}}$

$= 2^{-9} = \dfrac{1}{2^9} = \dfrac{1}{512}$

19. $\sqrt{\dfrac{8}{18}} = \sqrt{\dfrac{4 \cdot 2}{9 \cdot 2}} = \sqrt{\dfrac{4 \cdot \cancel{2}}{9 \cdot \cancel{2}}} = \sqrt{\dfrac{4}{9}} = \dfrac{\sqrt{4}}{\sqrt{9}} = \dfrac{2}{3}$

21. $\sqrt[3]{\dfrac{(27)(8)}{125}} = \sqrt[3]{\dfrac{216}{125}} = \dfrac{\sqrt[3]{216}}{\sqrt[3]{125}} = \dfrac{6}{5}$

Section 1.4: Solving Quadratic Equations Using the Quadratic Formula

1. $x^3 = 8$

$(x^3)^{1/3} = 8^{1/3}$

$x^{3 \cdot \frac{1}{3}} = \sqrt[3]{8}$

$x^{\frac{3}{3}} = 2$

$x = 2$

3. $y^4 = 81$

$(y^4)^{1/4} = \pm 81^{1/4}$

$(y^4)^{1/4} = \pm \sqrt[4]{81}$

$y^{4 \cdot \frac{1}{4}} = \pm 3$

$y^{\frac{4}{4}} = \pm 3$

$y = \pm 3$

5. $b^{-2} = \frac{1}{4}$

$(b^{-2})^{-1/2} = \pm \left(\frac{1}{4}\right)^{-1/2}$

$(b^{-2})^{-1/2} = \pm (4^{-1})^{-1/2}$

$b^{(-2)\left(-\frac{1}{2}\right)} = \pm 4^{1/2}$

$b^{\frac{2}{2}} = \pm \sqrt{4}$

$b = \pm 2$

7. $p^5 = 1.3$

$(p^5)^{1/5} = (1.3)^{1/5}$

$p^{5\left(\frac{1}{5}\right)} = (1.3)^{1/5}$

$p = 1.3^{1/5}$

9. $t^{9.3} = 9.3$

$(t^{9.3})^{1/9.3} = 9.3^{1/9.3}$

$t^{9.3/9.3} = 9.3^{1/9.3}$

$t = 9.3^{1/9.3}$

11. **Method 1: Solve by factoring.**

$(x - 3)(x - 2) = 0$

$x - 3 = 0 \quad or \quad x - 2 = 0$

$ + 3 \quad +3 +2 \quad +2$

$x = 3 \quad or \quad x = 2$

Method 2: Solve by the use of the Quadratic Formula.

$x^2 - 5x + 6 = 0$, where $a = 1, b = -5$, and $c = 6$.

$x = \dfrac{-b \pm \sqrt{b^2 - 4ac}}{2a} = \dfrac{-(-5) \pm \sqrt{(-5)^2 - 4(1)(6)}}{2(1)} = \dfrac{5 \pm \sqrt{25 - 24}}{2} = \dfrac{5 \pm \sqrt{1}}{2} = \dfrac{5 \pm 1}{2}$

$x = \dfrac{5 + 1}{2} = \dfrac{6}{2} = 3 \quad or \quad x = \dfrac{5 - 1}{2} = \dfrac{4}{2} = 2$

13. $2p^2 + 6p - 4 = 0$, where $a = 2, b = 6$, and $c = -4$.

$$p = \frac{-b \pm \sqrt{b^2 - 4ac}}{2a} = \frac{-6 \pm \sqrt{(6)^2 - 4(2)(-4)}}{2(2)} = \frac{-6 \pm \sqrt{36 + 32}}{4} = \frac{-6 \pm \sqrt{68}}{4} = \frac{-6 \pm \sqrt{4 \cdot 17}}{4}$$

$$= \frac{-6 \pm 2\sqrt{17}}{4} = \frac{2(-3 \pm \sqrt{17})}{4} = \frac{-3 \pm \sqrt{17}}{2}$$

$$p = \frac{-3 + \sqrt{17}}{2} \quad \text{or} \quad p = \frac{-3 - \sqrt{17}}{2}$$

15. **Method 1: Solve by factoring.**

$$(x + 3)(x + 3) = 0$$
$$x + 3 = 0$$
$$ -3 \quad -3$$
$$x = -3$$

Method 2: Solve by the use of the Quadratic Formula.

$x^2 + 6x + 9 = 0$, where $a = 1, b = 6$, and $c = 9$.

$$x = \frac{-b \pm \sqrt{b^2 - 4ac}}{2a} = \frac{-6 \pm \sqrt{(6)^2 - 4(1)(9)}}{2(1)} = \frac{-6 \pm \sqrt{36 - 36}}{2} = \frac{-6 \pm \sqrt{0}}{2} = \frac{-6}{2} = -3$$

17. **Method 1: Solve by factoring.**

$$(3n - 1)(n + 1) = 0$$
$$3n - 1 = 0 \qquad or \qquad n + 1 = 0$$
$$3n - 1 = 0 \qquad\qquad\quad -1 \quad -1$$
$$+1 \quad +1 \qquad\qquad n = -1$$
$$3n = 1$$
$$\frac{3n}{3} = \frac{1}{3}$$
$$n = \frac{1}{3}$$

Method 2: Solve by the use of the Quadratic Formula.

$3n^2 + 2n - 1 = 0$, where $a = 3, b = 2$, and $c = -1$.

$$n = \frac{-b \pm \sqrt{b^2 - 4ac}}{2a} = \frac{-2 \pm \sqrt{(2)^2 - 4(3)(-1)}}{2(3)} = \frac{-2 \pm \sqrt{4 + 12}}{6} = \frac{-2 \pm \sqrt{16}}{6} = \frac{-2 \pm 4}{6}$$

$$n = \frac{-2 + 4}{6} = \frac{2}{6} = \frac{1}{3} \quad \text{or} \quad n = \frac{-2 - 4}{6} = \frac{-6}{6} = -1$$

19. Before solving the equation for t, rewrite it into the standard quadratic form:

$at^2 + bt + c = 0.$

$5t^2 - t = 1$

$\quad\ \ -1 \ \ -1$

$5t^2 - t - 1 = 0$, where $a = 5, b = -1$, and $c = -1$.

$t = \dfrac{-b \pm \sqrt{b^2 - 4ac}}{2a} = \dfrac{-(-1) \pm \sqrt{(-1)^2 - 4(5)(-1)}}{2(5)} = \dfrac{1 \pm \sqrt{1 + 20}}{10} = \dfrac{1 \pm \sqrt{21}}{10}$

$t = \dfrac{1 + \sqrt{21}}{10}$ or $t = \dfrac{1 - \sqrt{21}}{10}$

21. **Method I: Solve by factoring.**

$x(x - 2) = 0$

$x = 0 \quad or \quad x - 2 = 0$

$\qquad\qquad\qquad\ +2 \quad +2$

$\qquad\qquad\qquad\ \ x = 2$

Method 2: Solve by the use of the Quadratic Formula.

$x^2 - 2x = 0$, where $a = 1, b = -2$, and $c = 0$.

$x = \dfrac{-b \pm \sqrt{b^2 - 4ac}}{2a} = \dfrac{-(-2) \pm \sqrt{(-2)^2 - 4(1)(0)}}{2(1)} = \dfrac{2 \pm \sqrt{4 - 0}}{2} = \dfrac{2 \pm \sqrt{4}}{2} = \dfrac{2 \pm 2}{2}$

$x = \dfrac{2 + 2}{2} = \dfrac{4}{2} = 2$ or $x = \dfrac{2 - 2}{2} = \dfrac{0}{2} = 0$

Section 1.5: The Cartesian Coordinate System

1. (a) A: $(3, 2)$, B: $(9, 6)$, C: $(10, 0)$, D: $(4, -6)$, E: $(8, -4)$, F: $(-6, 5)$, G: $(-2, 1)$

$\quad$ H: $(0, 5)$, I: $(-5, -3)$, J: $(-1, -4)$, K: $(0, -7)$

(b) Points A and B.

3. (a)

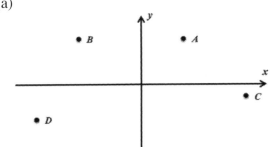

(b)

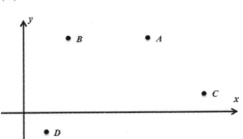

(c)

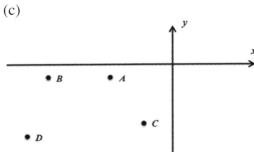

5.

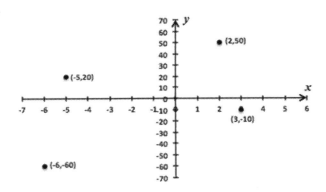

7. (a) The value of the y-coordinate for every point on the x-axis is 0.

   (b) The value of the x-coordinate for every point on the y-axis is 0.

9.

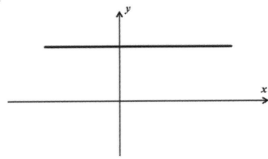

Every point on the line that is parallel to the x-axis has the same y-coordinate value.

Section 1.6: Graphical Solutions to Equations in Two Unknowns

1. If possible, solve the equation for y. We have:

$$2x - 3y = 5$$
$$\underline{-2x \qquad\quad -2x}$$
$$-3y = -2x + 5$$
$$\frac{-3y}{-3} = \frac{-2x+5}{-3}$$

$$y = \frac{-2x}{-3} + \frac{5}{-3}$$

$$y = \frac{2x}{3} - \frac{5}{3}$$

To graph the equation, choose arbitrary x-values and then, substitute each x-value into the equation to find its corresponding y-value. Then plot the points on a graph. We have:

For $x = -2$, $y = \dfrac{2(-2)}{3} - \dfrac{5}{3} = \dfrac{-4}{3} - \dfrac{5}{3} = \dfrac{-4-5}{3} = \dfrac{-9}{3} = -3.0$

For $x = -1$, $y = \dfrac{2(-1)}{3} - \dfrac{5}{3} = \dfrac{-2}{3} - \dfrac{5}{3} = \dfrac{-2-5}{3} = \dfrac{-7}{3} = -2.3$

For $x = -0.5$, $y = \dfrac{2(-0.5)}{3} - \dfrac{5}{3} = \dfrac{-1}{3} - \dfrac{5}{3} = \dfrac{-1-5}{3} = \dfrac{-6}{3} = -2.0$

For $x = 0$, $y = \dfrac{2(0)}{3} - \dfrac{5}{3} = 0 - \dfrac{5}{3} = -\dfrac{5}{3} = -1.7$

For $x = 0.5$, $y = \dfrac{2(0.5)}{3} - \dfrac{5}{3} = \dfrac{1}{3} - \dfrac{5}{3} = \dfrac{1-5}{3} = \dfrac{-4}{3} = -1.3$

For $x = 1$, $y = \dfrac{2(1)}{3} - \dfrac{5}{3} = \dfrac{2}{3} - \dfrac{5}{3} = \dfrac{2-5}{3} = \dfrac{-3}{3} = -1$

For $x = 2$, $y = \dfrac{2(2)}{3} - \dfrac{5}{3} = \dfrac{4}{3} - \dfrac{5}{3} = \dfrac{4-5}{3} = \dfrac{-1}{3} = -0.3$

x	y	(x, y)
-2	-3	$(-2, -3)$
-1	-2.3	$(-1, -2.3)$
-0.5	-2	$(-0.5, -2)$
0	-1.7	$(0, -1.7)$
0.5	-1.3	$(0.5, -1.3)$
1	-1	$(1, -1)$
2	-0.3	$(2, -0.3)$

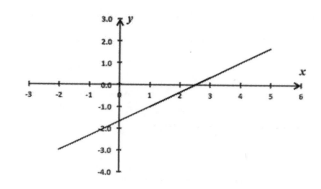

3. If possible, solve the equation for y. We have:

$$6x - 2y = 3$$
$$\underline{-6x \qquad\quad - 6x}$$
$$-2y = -6x + 3$$
$$\frac{-2y}{-2} = \frac{-6x+3}{-2}$$

$$y = \frac{-6x}{-2} + \frac{3}{-2}$$

$$y = 3x - \frac{3}{2}$$

To graph the equation, choose arbitrary x-values and then, substitute each x-value into the equation to find its corresponding y-value. Then plot the points on a graph. We have:

For $x = -2$, $y = 3(-2) - \frac{3}{2} = -6 - 1.5 = -6 + (-1.5) = -7.5$

For $x = -1$, $y = 3(-1) - \frac{3}{2} = -3 - \frac{3}{2} = -3 - 1.5 = -3 + (-1.5) = -4.5$

For $x = -0.5$, $y = 3(-0.5) - \frac{3}{2} = -1.5 - 1.5 = -1.5 + (-1.5) = -3.0$

For $x = 0$, $y = 3(0) - \frac{3}{2} = 0 - 1.5 = -1.5$

For $x = 0.5$, $y = 3(0.5) - \frac{3}{2} = 1.5 - 1.5 = 0$

For $x = 1$, $y = 3(1) - \frac{3}{2} = 3 - 1.5 = 1.5$

For $x = 2$, $y = 3(2) - \frac{3}{2} = 6 - 1.5 = 4.5$

x	y	(x, y)
-2	-7.5	$(-2, -7.5)$
-1	-4.5	$(-1, -4.5)$
-0.5	-3	$(-0.5, -3)$
0	-1.5	$(0, -1.5)$
0.5	0	$(0.5, 0)$
1	1.5	$(1, 1.5)$
2	4.5	$(2, 4.5)$

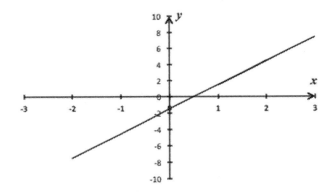

5. To graph the equation, choose arbitrary x-values and then, substitute each x-value into the equation to find its corresponding y-value. Then plot the points on a graph. We have:

For $x = -2$, $y = 2(-2)^2 = 2 \cdot 4 = 8$

For $x = -1$, $y = 2(-1)^2 = 2 \cdot 1 = 2$

For $x = -0.5$, $y = 2(-0.5)^2 = 2(.25) = 0.5$

For $x = 0$, $y = 2(0)^2 = 2 \cdot 0 = 0$

For $x = 1$, $y = 2(1)^2 = 2 \cdot 1 = 2$

For $x = 2$, $y = 2(2)^2 = 2 \cdot 4 = 8$

x	y	(x, y)
-2	8	$(-2, 8)$
-1	2	$(-1, 2)$
-0.5	0.5	$(-0.5, 0.5)$
0	0	$(0, 0)$
0.5	0.5	$(0.5, 0.5)$
1	2	$(1, 2)$
2	8	$(2, 8)$

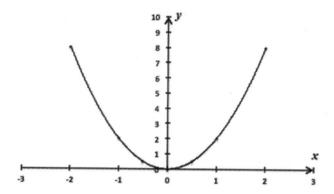

7. To graph the equation, choose arbitrary x-values and then, substitute each x-value into the equation to find its corresponding y-value. Then plot the points on a graph. We have:

For $x = -2$, $y = (-2)^3 - 2(-2)^2 + (-2) = -8 - 8 - 2 = -18$

For $x = -1$, $y = (-1)^3 - 2(-1)^2 + (-1) = -1 - 2 - 1 = -4$

For $x = -0.5$, $y = (-0.5)^3 - 2(-0.5)^2 + (-0.5) = -0.125 - 0.5 - 0.5 = -1.13$

For $x = 0$, $y = (0)^3 - 2(0)^2 + (0) = 0$

For $x = 0.5$, $y = (0.5)^3 - 2(0.5)^2 + 0.5 = 0.125 - 0.5 + 0.5 = 0.13$

For $x = 1$, $y = (1)^3 - 2(1)^2 + 1 = 1 - 2 + 1 = 0$

For $x = 2$, $y = (2)^3 - 2(2)^2 + 2 = 8 - 8 + 2 = 2$

x	$y = x^3 - 2x^2 + x$	(x, y)
-2	-18	$(-2, -18)$
-1	-4	$(-1, -4)$
-0.5	-1.13	$(-0.5, -1.13)$
0	0	$(0, 0)$
0.5	0.13	$(0.5, 0.13)$
1	0	$(1, 0)$
2	2	$(2, 2)$

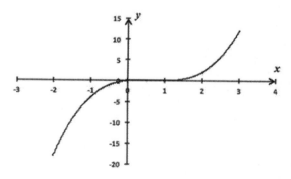

A close-up look at the graph of $y = x^3 - 2x^2 + x$ over the interval $[0, 1]$.

For $x = -1$, $y = (-1)^3 - 2(-1)^2 + (-1) = -1 - 2 - 1 = -4$

For $x = -0.5$, $y = (-0.5)^3 - 2(-0.5)^2 + (-0.5) = -0.125 - 0.5 - 0.5 = -1.13$

For $x = 0$, $y = (0)^3 - 2(0)^2 + (0) = 0$

For $x = 0.25$, $y = (0.25)^3 - 2(0.25)^2 + 0.25 = 0.015625 - 0.125 + 0.25 = 0.14$

For $x = 0.5$, $y = (0.5)^3 - 2(0.5)^2 + 0.5 = 0.125 - 0.5 + 0.5 = 0.13$

For $x = 0.56$, $y = (0.56)^3 - 2(0.56)^2 + 0.56 = 0.175616 - .6272 + 0.56 = 0.11$

For $x = 0.5$, $y = (0.75)^3 - 2(0.75)^2 + 0.75 = 0.421875 - 1.125 + 0.75 = 0.05$

For $x = 1$, $y = (1)^3 - 2(1)^2 + 1 = 1 - 2 + 1 = 0$

For $x = 2$, $y = (2)^3 - 2(2)^2 + 2 = 8 - 8 + 2 = 2$

x	$y = x^3 - 2x^2 + x$	(x, y)
-1	-4	$(-1, -4)$
-0.5	-1.13	$(-1, -1.13)$
0	0	$(0, 0)$
0.25	0.14	$(0.25, 0.14)$
0.5	0.13	$(0.5, 0.13)$
0.56	0.11	$(0.56, 0.11)$
0.75	0.05	$(0.75, 0.05)$
1	0	$(1, 0)$
2	2	$(2, 2)$

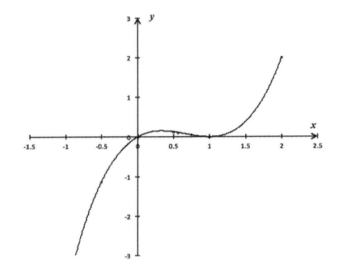

9. If possible, solve the equation for y. We have

$$x^2 + y^2 = 4$$
$$-x^2 \qquad - x^2$$

$$y^2 = 4 - x^2$$

$$y = \pm\sqrt{4 - x^2}$$

To graph the equation, choose arbitrary x-values and then, substitute each x-value into the equation to find its corresponding y-value. Then plot the points on a graph. We have:

For the equation: $y = \sqrt{4 - x^2}$.

For $x = -2$, $y = \sqrt{4 - (-2)^2} = \sqrt{4 - 4} = \sqrt{0} = 0$

For $x = -1.5$, $y = \sqrt{4 - (-1.5)^2} = \sqrt{4 - 2.25} = \sqrt{1.75} = 1.3$

For $x = -1.25$, $y = \sqrt{4 - (-1.25)^2} = \sqrt{4 - 1.6} = \sqrt{2.4} = 1.5$

For $x = -1$, $y = \sqrt{4 - (-1)^2} = \sqrt{4 - 1} = \sqrt{3} = 1.7$

For $x = -0.5$, $y = \sqrt{4 - (-0.5)^2} = \sqrt{4 - 0.25} = \sqrt{3.75} = 1.9$

For $x = 0$, $y = \sqrt{4 - 0^2} = \sqrt{4} = 2$

For $x = 0.5$, $y = \sqrt{4 - (0.5)^2} = \sqrt{4 - 0.25} = \sqrt{3.75} = 1.9$

For $x = 1$, $y = \sqrt{4 - (1)^2} = \sqrt{4 - 1} = \sqrt{3} = 1.7$

For $x = 1.25$, $y = \sqrt{4 - (1.25)^2} = \sqrt{4 - 1.6} = \sqrt{2.4} = 1.5$

For $x = 1.5$, $y = \sqrt{4 - (1.5)^2} = \sqrt{4 - 2.25} = \sqrt{1.75} = 1.3$

For $x = 2$, $y = \sqrt{4 - (2)^2} = \sqrt{4 - 4} = \sqrt{0} = 0$

For the equation: $y = -\sqrt{4 - x^2}$.

For $x = -2$, $y = -\sqrt{4 - (-2)^2} = -\sqrt{4 - 4} = \sqrt{0} = 0$

For $x = -1.5$, $y = -\sqrt{4 - (-1.5)^2} = -\sqrt{4 - 2.25} = -\sqrt{1.75} = -1.3$

For $x = -1.25$, $y = -\sqrt{4 - (-1.25)^2} = -\sqrt{4 - 1.6} = -\sqrt{2.4} = -1.5$

For $x = -1$, $y = -\sqrt{4 - (-1)^2} = -\sqrt{4 - 1} = -\sqrt{3} = -1.7$

For $x = -0.5$, $y = -\sqrt{4 - (-0.5)^2} = -\sqrt{4 - 0.25} = -\sqrt{3.75} = -1.9$

For $x = 0$, $y = -\sqrt{4 - 0^2} = -\sqrt{4} = -2$

For $x = 0.5$, $y = -\sqrt{4 - (0.5)^2} = -\sqrt{4 - 0.25} = -\sqrt{3.75} = -1.9$

For $x = 1$, $y = -\sqrt{4 - (1)^2} = -\sqrt{4 - 1} = -\sqrt{3} = -1.7$

For $x = 1.25$, $y = -\sqrt{4 - (1.25)^2} = -\sqrt{4 - 1.6} = -\sqrt{2.4} = -1.5$

For $x = 1.5$, $y = -\sqrt{4 - (1.5)^2} = -\sqrt{4 - 2.25} = -\sqrt{1.75} = -1.3$

For $x = 2$, $y = -\sqrt{4 - (2)^2} = -\sqrt{4 - 4} = \sqrt{0} = 0$

x	$y = \sqrt{4 - x^2}$	(x, y)
-2	0	$(-2, 0)$
-1.5	1.3	$(-1.5, 1.3)$
-1.25	1.5	$(-1.25, 1.5)$
-1	1.7	$(-1, 1.7)$
-0.5	1.9	$(-0.5, 1.9)$
0	2	$(0, 0)$
0.5	1.9	$(0.5, 1.9)$
1	1.7	$(1, 1.7)$
1.25	1.5	$(1.25, 1.5)$
1.5	1.3	$(1.5, 1.3)$
2	0	$(2, 0)$

x	$y = -\sqrt{4 - x^2}$	(x, y)
-2	0	$(-2, 0)$
-1.5	-1.3	$(-1.5, -1.3)$
-1.25	-1.5	$(-1.25, -1.5)$
-1	-1.7	$(-1, -1.7)$
-0.5	-1.9	$(-0.5, -1.9)$
0	-2	$(0, -2)$
0.5	-1.9	$(0.5, -1.9)$
1	-1.7	$(1, -1.7)$
1.25	-1.5	$(1.25, -1.5)$
1.5	-1.3	$(1.5, -1.3)$
2	0	$(2, 0)$

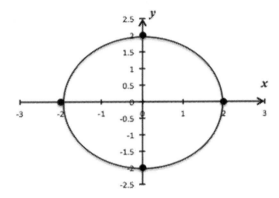

11.

x	$y = x$	(x, y)
-3	-3	$(-3, -3)$
-2	-2	$(-2, -2)$
-1	-1	$(-1, -1)$
-0.5	-0.5	$(-0.5, -0.5)$
0	0	$(0, 0)$
0.5	0.5	$(0.5, 0.5)$
1	1	$(1, 1)$
2	2	$(2, 2)$
3	3	$(3, 3)$

x	$y = -x$	(x, y)
-3	3	$(-3, 3)$
-2	2	$(-2, 2)$
-1	1	$(-1, 1)$
-0.5	0.5	$(-0.5, -0.5)$
0	0	$(0, 0)$
0.5	-0.5	$(0.5, -0.5)$
1	-1	$(1, -1)$
2	-2	$(2, -2)$
3	-3	$(3, -3)$

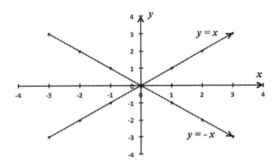

The lines have opposite slopes.

13. The points lie on the graph if they satisfy the equation $y = 3x^2 + 4x + 2$.

For $x = -2$, $y = 3(-2)^2 + 4(-2) + 2 = 3 \cdot 4 - 8 + 2 = 12 - 8 + 2 = 6$.

Therefore, $(-2, 6)$ is on the graph of $y = 3x^2 + 4x + 2$.

For $x = 0$, $y = 3(0)^2 + 4(0) + 2 = 3 \cdot 0 + 0 + 2 = 2$. Therefore, $(0, 2)$ is on the graph of $y = 3x^2 + 4x + 2$.

For $x = 1$, $y = 3(1)^2 + 4(1) + 2 = 3 \cdot 1 + 4 + 2 = 3 + 4 + 2 = 9$. Therefore, $(1, 9)$ is on the graph of $y = 3x^2 + 4x + 2$.

Hence, all three points lie on the graph of $y = 3x^2 + 4x + 2$.

15. **(A) Solve by Graphing**

To graph the equation, choose arbitrary x-values and then, substitute each x-value into the equation to find its corresponding y-value. Then plot the points on a graph. We have:

For the equation $y = 5x^2 - 2$:

For $x = -2$, $y = 5(-2)^2 - 2 = 5 \cdot 4 - 2 = 20 - 2 = 18$

For $x = -1.5$, $y = 5(-1.5)^2 - 2 = 11.25 - 2 = 9.25$

For $x = -1$, $y = 5(-1)^2 - 2 = 5 \cdot 1 - 2 = 5 - 2 = 3$

For $x = -0.5$, $y = 5(-0.5)^2 - 2 = 1.25 - 2 = -0.75$

For $x = 0$, $y = 5(0)^2 - 2 = 5 \cdot 0 - 2 = 0 - 2 = -2$

For $x = 0.5$, $y = 5(0.5)^2 - 2 = 1.25 - 2 = -0.75$

For $x = 1$, $y = 5(1)^2 - 2 = 5 \cdot 1 - 2 = 5 - 2 = 3$

For $x = 1.5$, $y = 5(1.5)^2 - 2 = 11.25 - 2 = 9.25$

For $x = 2$, $y = 5(2)^2 - 2 = 5 \cdot 4 - 2 = 20 - 2 = 18$

For the equation $y = x + 3$:

For $x = -2$, $y = -2 + 3 = 1$

For $x = -1.5$, $y = -1.5 + 3 = 1.5$

For $x = -1$, $y = -1 + 3 = 2$

For $x = -0.5$, $y = -0.5 + 3 = 2.5$

For $x = 0$, $y = 0 + 3 = 3$

For $x = 0.5$, $y = 0.5 + 3 = 3.5$

For $x = 1$, $y = 1 + 3 = 4$

For $x = 1.5$, $y = 1.5 + 3 = 4.5$

For $x = 2$, $y = 2 + 3 = 5$

x	$y = 5x^2 - 2$	(x, y)
-2	18	$(-2, 18)$
-1.5	9.25	$(-1.5, 9.25)$
-1	3	$(-1, 3)$
-0.5	-0.75	$(-0.5, -0.75)$
0	-2	$(0, -2)$
0.5	-0.75	$(0.5, -0.75)$
1	3	$(1, 3)$
1.5	9.25	$(1.5, 9.25)$
2	18	$(2, 18)$

x	$y = x + 3$	(x, y)
-2	1	$(-2, 1)$
-1.5	1.5	$(-1.5, 1.5)$
-1	2	$(-1, 2)$
-0.5	2.5	$(-0.5, 2.5)$
0	3	$(0, 3)$
0.5	3.5	$(0.5, 3.5)$
1	4	$(1, 4)$
1.5	4.5	$(1.5, 4.5)$
2	5	$(2, 5)$

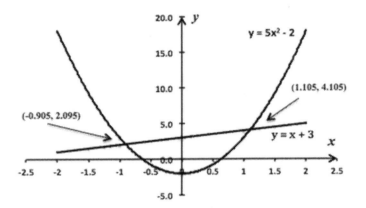

(B) Solve Algebraically

To find the points of intersection, we have to solve the system of equations:

(1) $y = 5x^2 - 2$
(2) $y = x + 3$

Using the Substitution Method, substitute y (as $x + 3$) in equation (1) into equation (2). We have:

$5x^2 - 2 = x + 3$

$-x - 3 \qquad -x - 3$

$5x^2 - 2 - x - 3 = 0$

$5x^2 - x - 5 = 0.$

Use the Quadratic Formula with $a = 5, b = -1,$ and $c = -5$ to solve for x. We have:

$$x = \frac{-b \pm \sqrt{b^2 - 4ac}}{2a} = \frac{-(-1) \pm \sqrt{(-1)^2 - 4(5)(-5)}}{2(5)} = \frac{1 \pm \sqrt{1 + 100}}{10} = \frac{1 \pm \sqrt{101}}{10}$$

Therefore, $x_1 = \dfrac{1 + \sqrt{101}}{10} = 1.105$ or $x_2 = \dfrac{1 - \sqrt{101}}{10} = -0.905$

We now need to find the y components for these x-values. We can use either equation (1) or (2) to find y. The results will be the same. Let's choose equation (2) since it is simpler.

For $x = 1.105$, $y = 1.105 + 3 = 4.105$.

For $x = -0.905$, $y = -0.905 + 3 = 2.095$.

Points of intersection: $(1.105, 4.105)$ and $(-0.905, 2.095)$

Section 1.7: Sigma Notation

1. (a) $\displaystyle\sum_{i=1}^{3}(x_i)^2 = x_1^2 + x_2^2 + x_3^2$

(b) $\displaystyle\sum_{i=3}^{11} 2x_i = 2x_3 + 2x_4 + 2x_5 + 2x_6 + 2x_7 + 2x_8 + 2x_9 + 2x_{10} + 2x_{11}$

(c) $\displaystyle\sum_{i=1}^{6}(x_i + y_i) = (x_1 + y_1) + (x_2 + y_2) + (x_3 + y_3) + (x_4 + y_4) + (x_5 + y_5) + (x_6 + y_6)$

(d) $\displaystyle\sum_{j=99}^{105}(3M_j + 4)$

$= (3M_{99} + 4) + (3M_{100} + 4) + (3M_{101} + 4) + (3M_{102} + 4) + (3M_{103} + 4) + (3M_{104} + 4) + (3M_{105} + 4)$

3. (a) $\displaystyle\sum_{i=2}^{29}(3i)^2$ 　　　　(c) $\displaystyle\sum_{i=2}^{29} 2(3)^i$

(b) $\displaystyle\sum_{i=2}^{29} i(3^2)$ 　　　　(d) $\displaystyle\sum_{i=2}^{29}(-1)^i 3i^2$

5. (a) $\displaystyle\sum x_i = x_1 + x_2 + x_3 + x_4 + x_5 + x_6 = 0 + 8 + (-2) + 5 + (-3) + 7 = 15$

(b) $\displaystyle\sum y_i = y_1 + y_2 + y_3 + y_4 + y_5 + y_6 = 3 + 2 + 6 + 9 + 10 + 1 = 31$

(c) $\displaystyle\sum (x_i)^2 = (x_1)^2 + (x_2)^2 + (x_3)^2 + (x_4)^2 + (x_5)^2 + (x_6)^2$

$= (0)^2 + (8)^2 + (-2)^2 + (5)^2 + (-3)^2 + (7)^2$

$= 0 + 64 + 4 + 25 + 9 + 49 = 151$

(d) $\sum(x_i - 2) = (x_1 - 2) + (x_2 - 2) + (x_3 - 2) + (x_4 - 2) + (x_5 - 2) + (x_6 - 2)$

$= (0 - 2) + (8 - 2) + (-2 - 2) + (5 - 2) + (-3 - 2) + (7 - 2)$

$= -2 + 6 + (-4) + 3 + (-5) + 5 = 3$

(e) $\sum(x_i y_i) = (x_1 y_1) + (x_2 y_2) + (x_3 y_3) + (x_4 y_4) + (x_5 y_5) + (x_6 y_6)$

$= (0)(3) + (8)(2) + (-2)(6) + (5)(9) + (-3)(10) + (7)(1)$

$= 0 + 16 - 12 + 45 - 30 + 7 = 26$

(f) $\left(\sum x_i\right)\left(\sum y_i\right) = (x_1 + x_2 + x_3 + x_4 + x_5 + x_6)(y_1 + y_2 + y_3 + y_4 + y_5 + y_6)$

$= (0 + 8 + (-2) + 5 + (-3) + 7)(3 + 2 + 6 + 9 + 10 + 1) = (15)(31) = 465$

(g) The sums are not equal. Therefore, $\sum(x_i y_i) \neq \left(\sum x_i\right)\left(\sum y_i\right)$

7. (a) $c\left(\sum_{i=1}^{n} x_i\right) = c(x_1 + x_2 + x_3 + \cdots + x_n)$.

Using the distributive property, we have:

$= cx_i + cx_2 + cx_3 + \cdots + cx_n = \sum_{i=1}^{n}(cx_i)$

(b) $\sum_{i=1}^{n}(x_i + y_i) = (x_1 + y_1) + (x_2 + y_2) + (x_3 + y_3) + \cdots + (x_n + y_n)$.

Dropping the parenthesis, we have:

$= x_i + y_1 + x_2 + y_2 + x_3 + y_3 + \cdots + x_n + y_n$

Because addition is commutative, we can rearrange the terms and the sum will still be the same. We have:

$= x_1 + x_2 + x_3 + \cdots + x_n + y_1 + y_2 + y_3 + \cdots + y_n$

$= (x_1 + x_2 + x_3 + \cdots + x_n) + (y_1 + y_2 + y_3 + \cdots + y_n)$

$= \sum_{i=1}^{n}(x_i) + \sum_{i=1}^{n}(y_i)$

(c) $\displaystyle\sum_{i=1}^{m} x_i + \sum_{i=m+1}^{n} x_i = x_1 + x_2 + x_3 + \cdots + x_m + x_{m+1} + x_{m+2} + \cdots + x_n = \sum_{i=1}^{n} x_i$

9. $\displaystyle average = \frac{G_1 + G_2 + G_3 + \cdots + G_n}{n} = \frac{1}{n}\sum_{i=1}^{n} G_i$

Section 1.8: Numerical Considerations

1. $\frac{2}{3} = 0.\overline{6} \approx 0.67$

3. $\frac{4}{17} = 0.235294117647 \approx 0.24$

5. $\frac{89}{31} = 2.87096774194 \approx 2.87$

7. $\frac{2}{3} = 0.\overline{6} \approx 0.667$

$\frac{4}{11} = 0.\overline{36} \approx 0.364$

$\frac{4}{17} = 0.235294117647 \approx 0.235$

$\frac{12}{7} = 1.71428571429 \approx 1.714$

$\frac{89}{31} = 2.87096774194 \approx 2.871$

9. $3.35642\ E3 = 3{,}356.42$

11. $3.356\ E\text{-}3 = .003356$

13. $3.3\ E12 = 3{,}300{,}000{,}000{,}000$

Chapter 2 Equations and Graphs

Section 2.1: Linear Equations

1. If possible, rewrite equations (a) – (j) in the standard form: $Ax + By = C$.

(a) $2x = y$

$\quad -y \quad -y$

$\quad 2x - y = 0$

We see that it is in the form $Ax + By = C$, with $A = 2, B = -1$, and $C = 0$. Therefore, the given equation is linear.

(b) $2x = \dfrac{1}{y}$

$\quad 2x = y^{-1}$

$\quad -y^{-1} \quad -y^{-1}$

$\quad 2x - y^{-1} = 0$

Because the exponent on y is -1 instead of 1, the given equation is not linear.

(c) $xy = 4$

$\quad \dfrac{xy}{y} = \dfrac{4}{y}$, for $y \neq 0$

$\quad x = \dfrac{4}{y}$

$\quad x = 4y^{-1}$

$\quad -4y^{-1} \quad -4y^{-1}$
$\quad x - 4y^{-1} = 0$

Because the exponent on y is -1 instead of 1, the given equation is not linear.

(d) Rewriting $x = 4$ as $x + 0y = 4$, we see that it is in the form $Ax + By = C$, with $A = 1, B = 0$, and $C = 4$. Therefore, the given equation is linear.

(e) $2x - 3y = 0$

We see that it is in the form $Ax + By = C$, with $A = 2, B = -3$, and $C = 0$. Therefore, the given equation is linear.

(f) $y = 4x$

$\quad -4x \quad -4x$

$\quad -4x + y = 0$

We see that it is in the form $Ax + By = C$, with $A = -4, B = 1$, and $C = 0$. Therefore, the given equation is linear.

(g) $y = 4x^2$

$\quad -4x^2 \quad - 4x^2$

$\quad -4x^2 + y = 0$

Because the exponent on x is 2 instead of 1, the given equation is not linear.

(h) $\quad x - 2 = 3y$

$\quad\quad -3y \quad\quad - 3y$

$\quad\quad x - 3y - 2 = 0$

$\quad\quad\quad\quad\quad +2 \quad +2$

$\quad\quad x - 3y = 2$

We see that it is in the form $Ax + By = C$, with $A = 1, B = -3$, and $C = 2$. Therefore, the given equation is linear.

(i) $\dfrac{1}{x} + \dfrac{1}{y} = 2$

$\quad x^{-1} + y^{-1} = 2$

Because the exponents on x *and* y are –1 instead of 1, the given equation is not linear.

(j) $\quad x = y$

$\quad\quad -y \quad - y$

$\quad\quad x - y = 0$

We see that it is in the form $Ax + By = C$, with $A = 1, B = -1$, and $C = 0$. Therefore, the given equation is linear.

3. **Part 1:** $\quad V = 6{,}000 - 1{,}500t$

Part 2: $\quad V = 6{,}000 - 1{,}500t$

$\quad\quad\quad +1{,}500t \quad\quad + 1{,}500t$

$\quad\quad\quad V + 1500t = 6{,}000$

We see that it is in the form $Ax + By = C$, with $A = 1, B = 1500$, and $C = 6{,}000$. Therefore, the given equation is linear.

Section 2.2: Graphing Linear Equations

1. If possible, solve equations (a) – (h) for y. To graph the equation, choose arbitrary x-values and then, substitute each x-value into the equation to find its corresponding y-value. Then, plot these points on a graph. We have:

(a) $2x + 3y = 6$
$-2x - 2x$

$\qquad y = \dfrac{-2x}{3} + \dfrac{6}{3}$

$3y = -2x + 6$

$\qquad y = -\dfrac{2}{3}x + 2$

$\dfrac{3y}{3} = \dfrac{-2x+6}{3}$

For $x = -3,\ y = \dfrac{-2(-3)}{3} + 2 = \dfrac{6}{3} + 2 = 2 + 2 = 4$

For $x = -2,\ y = \dfrac{-2(-2)}{3} + 2 = \dfrac{4}{3} + 2 = \dfrac{4}{3} + \dfrac{6}{3} = \dfrac{10}{3} = 3.33$

For $x = -1,\ y = \dfrac{-2(-1)}{3} + 2 = \dfrac{2}{3} + 2 = \dfrac{2}{3} + \dfrac{6}{3} = \dfrac{8}{3} = 2.67$

For $x = 0,\ y = \dfrac{-2(0)}{3} + 2 = 0 + 2 = 2$

For $x = 1,\ y = \dfrac{-2(1)}{3} + 2 = \dfrac{-2}{3} + 2 = \dfrac{-2}{3} + \dfrac{6}{3} = \dfrac{4}{3} = 1.33$

For $x = 2,\ y = \dfrac{-2(2)}{3} + 2 = \dfrac{-4}{3} + 2 = \dfrac{-4}{3} + \dfrac{6}{3} = \dfrac{2}{3} = 0.67$

For $x = 3,\ y = \dfrac{-2(3)}{3} + 2 = \dfrac{-6}{3} + 2 = -2 + 2 = 0$

x	$y = \dfrac{-2}{3}x+2$	(x, y)
-3	4	$(-3, 4)$
-2	3.33	$(-2, 3.33)$
-1	2.67	$(-1, 2.67)$
0	2	$(0, 2)$
1	1.33	$(1, 1.33)$
2	0.67	$(2, 0.67)$
3	0	$(3, 0)$

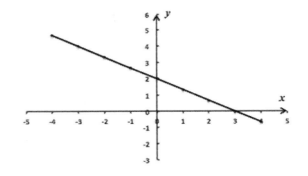

(b) $-2x + 3y = 6$
$+2x + 2x$

$\qquad y = \dfrac{2x}{3} + \dfrac{6}{3}$

$3y = 2x + 6$

$\qquad y = \dfrac{2}{3}x + 2$

$\dfrac{3y}{3} = \dfrac{2x+6}{3}$

For $x = -3, y = \dfrac{2(-3)}{3} + 2 = \dfrac{-6}{3} + 2 = -2 + 2 = 0$

For $x = -2, y = \dfrac{2(-2)}{3} + 2 = -\dfrac{4}{3} + \dfrac{6}{3} = \dfrac{-4+6}{3} = \dfrac{2}{3} = 0.67$

For $x = -1, y = \frac{2(-1)}{3} + 2 = \frac{-2}{3} + \frac{6}{3} = \frac{-2+6}{3} = \frac{4}{3} = 1.33$

For $x = 0, y = \frac{2(0)}{3} + 2 = 0 + 2 = 2$

For $x = 1, y = \frac{2(1)}{3} + 2 = \frac{2}{3} + 2 = \frac{2}{3} + \frac{6}{3} = \frac{8}{3} = 2.67$

For $x = 2, y = \frac{2(2)}{3} + 2 = \frac{4}{3} + 2 = \frac{4}{3} + \frac{6}{3} = \frac{10}{3} = 3.33$

For $x = 3, y = \frac{2(3)}{3} + 2 = \frac{6}{3} + 2 = 2 + 2 = 4$

x	$y = \frac{2}{3}x+2$	(x,y)
-3	0	$(-3, 0)$
-2	0.67	$(-2, 0.67)$
-1	1.33	$(-1, 1.33)$
0	2	$(0, 2)$
1	2.67	$(1, 2.67)$
2	3.33	$(2, 3.33)$
3	4	$(3, 4)$

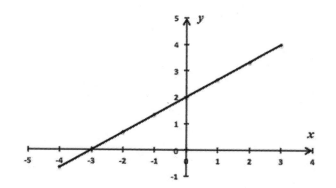

(c) $2x - 3y = 6$

$\quad -2x \qquad -2x$

$\quad -3y = -2x + 6$

$\quad \frac{-3y}{-3} = \frac{-2x+6}{-3}$

$y = \frac{-2x}{-3} + \frac{6}{-3}$

$y = \frac{2}{3}x - 2$

For $x = -3, y = \frac{2(-3)}{3} - 2 = \frac{-6}{3} - 2 = -2 - 2 = -4$

For $x = -2, y = \frac{2(-2)}{3} - 2 = \frac{-4}{3} - 2 = \frac{-4}{3} - \frac{6}{3} = -\frac{10}{3} = -3.33$

For $x = -1, y = \frac{2(-1)}{3} - 2 = \frac{-2}{3} - 2 = \frac{-2}{3} - \frac{6}{3} = -\frac{8}{3} = -2.67$

For $x = 0, y = \frac{2(0)}{3} - 2 = 0 - 2 = -2$

For $x = 1, y = \frac{2(1)}{3} - 2 = \frac{2}{3} - 2 = \frac{2}{3} - \frac{6}{3} = -\frac{4}{3} = -1.33$

For $x = 2, y = \frac{2(2)}{3} - 2 = \frac{4}{3} - 2 = \frac{4}{3} - \frac{6}{3} = -\frac{2}{3} = -0.67$

For $x = 3, y = \frac{2(3)}{3} - 2 = \frac{6}{3} - 2 = \frac{6}{3} - \frac{6}{3} = 0$

x	$y = \frac{2x}{3} - 2$	(x, y)
− 3	−4	$(-3, -4)$
−2	−3.33	$(-2, -3.33)$
−1	−2.67	$(-1, -2.67)$
0	0	$(0, -2)$
1	−1.33	$(1, -1.33)$
2	−0.67	$(2, -0.67)$
3	0	$(3, 0)$

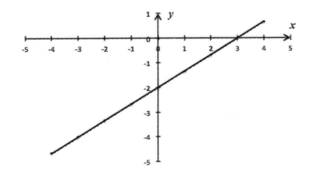

(d) $2x + 3y = -6$

$\quad -2x \qquad - 2x$

$\quad 3y = -2x - 6$

$\quad \dfrac{3y}{3} = \dfrac{-2x-6}{3}$

$$y = \frac{-2x}{3} - \frac{6}{3}$$

$$y = -\frac{2}{3}x - 2$$

For $x = -3, y = \dfrac{-2(-3)}{3} - 2 = \dfrac{6}{3} - 2 = 2 - 2 = 0$

For $x = -2, y = \dfrac{-2(-2)}{3} - 2 = \dfrac{4}{3} - 2 = \dfrac{4}{3} - \dfrac{6}{3} = -\dfrac{2}{3} = -0.67$

For $x = -1, y = \dfrac{-2(-1)}{3} - 2 = \dfrac{2}{3} - 2 = \dfrac{2}{3} - \dfrac{6}{3} = -\dfrac{4}{3} = -1.33$

For $x = 0, y = \dfrac{-2(0)}{3} - 2 = 0 - 2 = -2$

For $x = 1, y = \dfrac{-2(1)}{3} - 2 = \dfrac{-2}{3} - 2 = \dfrac{-2}{3} - \dfrac{6}{3} = -\dfrac{8}{3} = -2.67$

For $x = 2, y = \dfrac{-2(2)}{3} - 2 = \dfrac{-4}{3} - 2 = \dfrac{-4}{3} - \dfrac{6}{3} = -\dfrac{10}{3} = -3.33$

For $x = 3, y = \dfrac{-2(3)}{3} - 2 = \dfrac{-6}{3} - 2 = -2 - 2 = -4$

x	$y = -\dfrac{2}{3}x - 2$	(x, y)
− 3	0	$(-3, 0)$
− 2	−0.67	$(-2, -0.67)$
− 1	−1.33	$(-1, -1.33)$
0	−2	$(0, -2)$
1	−2.67	$(1, -2.67)$
2	−3.33	$(2, -3.33)$
3	−4	$(3, -4)$

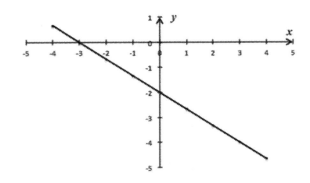

(e) $3x + 2y = 6$

$-3x -3x$

$2y = -3x + 6$

$\dfrac{2y}{2} = \dfrac{-3x+6}{2}$

$y = \dfrac{-3x}{2} + \dfrac{6}{2}$

$y = -\dfrac{3}{2}x + 3$

For $x = -3$, $y = \dfrac{-3(-3)}{2} + 3 = \dfrac{9}{2} + 3 = \dfrac{9}{2} + \dfrac{6}{2} = \dfrac{15}{2} = 7.5$

For $x = -2$, $y = \dfrac{-3(-2)}{2} + 3 = \dfrac{6}{2} + 3 = 3 + 3 = 6$

For $x = -1$, $y = \dfrac{-3(-1)}{2} + 3 = \dfrac{3}{2} + 3 = \dfrac{3}{2} + \dfrac{6}{2} = \dfrac{9}{2} = 4.5$

For $x = 0$, $y = \dfrac{-30}{2} + 3 = 0 + 3 = 3$

For $x = 1$, $y = \dfrac{-3(1)}{2} + 3 = \dfrac{-3}{2} + \dfrac{6}{2} = \dfrac{3}{2} = 1.5$

For $x = 2$, $y = \dfrac{-3(2)}{2} + 3 = \dfrac{-6}{2} + 3 = -3 + 3 = 0$

For $x = 3$, $y = \dfrac{-3(3)}{2} + 3 = \dfrac{-9}{2} + \dfrac{6}{2} = \dfrac{-9+6}{2} = \dfrac{-3}{2} - 1.5$

x	$y = -\frac{3}{2}x+3$	(x, y)
-3	7.5	$(-3, 7.5)$
-2	6	$(-2, 6)$
-1	4.5	$(-1, 4.5)$
0	3	$(0, 3)$
1	1.5	$(1, 1.5)$
2	0	$(2, 0)$
3	-1.5	$(3, -1.5)$

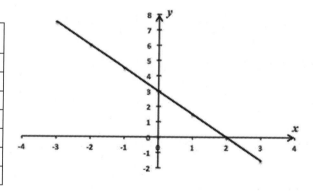

(f) $x = 7$ is a vertical line through the point $(7, 0)$.

x	y	(x, y)
7	-2	$(7, -2)$
7	-1	$(7, -1)$
7	0	$(7, 0)$
7	1	$(7, 1)$
7	2	$(7, 2)$
7	3	$(7, 3)$
7	4	$(7, 4)$

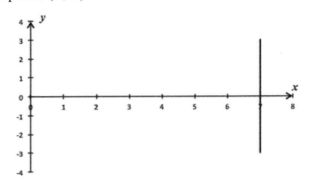

(g) $10x - 5y = 50$

$\quad -10x \qquad -10x$

$\quad -5y = -10x + 50$

$$\frac{-5y}{-5} = \frac{-10x + 50}{-5}$$

$$y = \frac{-10x}{-5} + \frac{50}{-5}$$

$$y = 2x - 10$$

For $x = -3, y = 2(-3) - 10 = -6 - 10 = -16$

For $x = -2, y = 2(-2) - 10 = -4 - 10 = -14$

For $x = -1, y = 2(-1) - 10 = -2 - 10 = -12$

For $x = 0, y = 2(0) - 10 = 0 - 10 = -10$

For $x = 1, y = 2(1) - 10 = 2 - 10 = -8$

For $x = 2, y = 2(2) - 10 = 4 - 10 = -6$

For $x = 3, y = 2(3) - 10 = 6 - 10 = -4$

x	$y = 2x - 10$	(x, y)
-3	-16	$(-3, -16)$
-2	-14	$(-2, -14)$
-1	-12	$(-1, -12)$
0	-10	$(0, -10)$
1	-8	$(1, -8)$
2	-6	$(2, -6)$
3	-4	$(3, -4)$

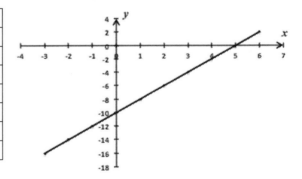

(h) $x = y$ or $y = x$

x	$y = x$	(x, y)
-3	-3	$(-3, -3)$
-2	-2	$(-2, -2)$
-1	-1	$(-1, -1)$
0	0	$(0, 0)$
1	1	$(1, 1)$
2	2	$(2, 2)$
3	3	$(3, 3)$

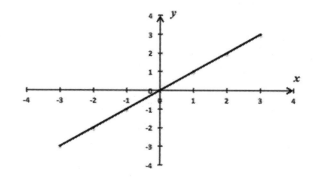

3. Given $S = 10$, we are to determine E. Substituting $S = 10$ into the given equation and solve for E. We have:

$$10 = 2E + 2.14$$
$$-2.14 \qquad -2.14$$
$$7.86 = 2E$$

$$\frac{7.86}{2} = \frac{2E}{2}$$
$$E = \$3.93 \; million$$

5. The price, p, at which the number of cans ceased to be saleable is when $A = 0$. That is,

$$0 = 200 - p$$
$$+p \qquad +p$$
$$p = 200 \; cents$$

Section 2.3: Properties of Straight Lines

1. If possible, rewrite equations (a) – (h) in the form: $y = mx + b$.

(a) $2x + 3y = 6$

$$-2x \qquad -2x$$
$$3y = -2x + 6$$
$$\frac{3y}{3} = \frac{-2x+6}{3}$$

$$y = \frac{-2x}{3} + \frac{6}{3}$$
$$y = -\frac{2}{3}x + 2.$$

Therefore, the slope $m = -\frac{2}{3}$

(b) $-2x + 3y = 6$

$$+2x \qquad +2x$$
$$3y = 2x + 6$$
$$\frac{3y}{3} = \frac{2x+6}{3}$$

$$y = \frac{2x}{3} + \frac{6}{3}$$
$$y = \frac{2}{3}x + 2.$$

Therefore, the slope $m = \frac{2}{3}$

(c) $2x - 3y = 6$

$\quad -2x \qquad -2x$

$\quad -3y = -2x + 6$

$$\frac{-3y}{-3} = \frac{-2x+6}{-3}$$

$$y = \frac{-2x}{-3} + \frac{6}{-3}$$

$$y = \frac{2}{3}x - 2$$

Therefore, the slope $m = \frac{2}{3}$.

(d) $2x + 3y = -6$

$\quad -2x \qquad -2x$

$\quad 3y = -2x - 6$

$$\frac{3y}{3} = \frac{-2x-6}{3}$$

$$y = \frac{-2x}{3} - \frac{6}{3}$$

$$y = -\frac{2}{3}x - 2$$

Therefore, the slope $m = -\frac{2}{3}$

(e) $3x + 2y = 6$

$\quad -3x \qquad -3x$

$\quad 2y = -3x + 6$

$$\frac{2y}{2} = \frac{-3x+6}{2}$$

$$y = \frac{-3x}{2} + \frac{6}{2}$$

$$y = -\frac{3}{2}x + 3$$

Therefore, the slope $m = -\frac{3}{2}$.

(g) $10x - 5y = 50$

$\quad -10x \qquad -10x$

$\quad -5y = -10x + 50$

$$\frac{-5y}{-5} = \frac{-10x+50}{-5}$$

$$y = \frac{-10x}{-5} + \frac{50}{-5}$$

$$y = 2x - 10$$

Therefore, the slope $m = 2$.

(f) $x = 7$ is a vertical line through the point $(7, 0)$. Therefore, it's slope is undefined or ∞.

(h) $x = y$ or $y = x + 0$

Therefore, the slope $m = 1$.

3. Let $t = 0$ stands for January, $t = 1$ for February, and so on. Then the y-intercept of the line is $(0, 1)$ and another point on the line is $(11, 3)$. Using $m = \frac{y_2-y_1}{x_2-x_1}$ with $(x_1, y_1) = (0,1)$ and $(x_2, y_2) = (11, 3)$, we have:

$$m = \frac{y_2-y_1}{x_2-x_1} = \frac{3-1}{11-0} = \frac{2}{11}$$

We are given the y-intercept $(0,1)$. Therefore, the equation relating attendance, A, to time t (in months) is $A = \frac{2}{11}t + 1$.

5. **Part 1**:

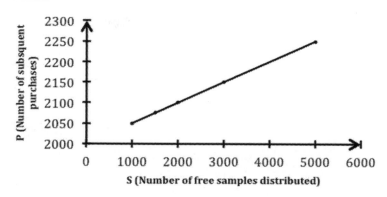

Part 2: The graph in **Part 1** indicates a straight-line relationship between P and S. So, we seek an equation of the form $P = mS + b$. Using $m = \frac{y_2 - y_1}{x_2 - x_1}$ with $(x_1, y_1) = (1000, 2050)$ and $(x_2, y_2) = (2000, 2100)$, we have:

$$m = \frac{y_2 - y_1}{x_2 - x_1} = \frac{2100 - 2050}{2000 - 1000} = \frac{50}{1000} = \frac{1}{20} = 0.05$$

To obtain b, we substitute any one of the data points, say $S = 1{,}000$ and $P = 2{,}050$ into $P = 0.05S + b$. We have:

$$2{,}050 = 0.05(1{,}000) + b$$
$$2{,}050 = 50 + b$$
$$-50 \quad -50$$
$$b = 2{,}000$$

Therefore, $P = \frac{1}{20}S + 2{,}000$ or $P = 0.05S + 2{,}000$

Section 2.4: Break-Even Analysis

1. (a) $C = ax + F$
   $C = 10x + 20{,}000$

   (b) $R = px$
   $R = 12x$

   (c) $P = Revenue - Cost = R - C$

   $$P = 12x - (10x + 20{,}000) = 12x - 10x - 20{,}000 = 2x - 20{,}000$$

   For $x = 3{,}000$, $P = 2(3{,}000) - 20{,}000 = 6{,}000 - 20{,}000 = -\$14{,}000$.

(d) $BEP = x = \dfrac{F}{p-a} = \dfrac{\$20,000}{\$12-\$10} = \dfrac{\$20,000}{\$2} = 10,000$ textbooks

3. **Algebraically**: $BEP = x = \dfrac{F}{p-a} = \dfrac{\$15,000}{\$12-\$2} = \dfrac{\$15,000}{\$10} = 1,500$ staplers

Graphically: To graph the equations $R = 12x$ and $C = 2x + 15,000$, choose arbitrary x-values and then, substitute each x-value into the equation to find its corresponding y-value. Then plot the points on a graph. We have:

For the equation: $y = R = 12x$

For $x = 0,\ y = 12(0) = 0$

For $x = 500,\ y = 12(500) = 6,000$

For $x = 1,000,\ y = 12(1,000) = 12,000$

For $x = 1,500,\ y = 12(1,500) = 18,000$

For $x = 2,000,\ y = 12(2,000) = 24,000$

For the equation: $y = C = 2x + 15,000$

For $x = 0,\qquad y = 2(0) + 15000 = 15,000$

For $x = 500,\quad y = 2(500) + 15000 = 1,000 + 15,000 = 16,000$

For $x = 1,000,\ y = 2(1,000) + 15000 = 2,000 + 15,000 = 17,000$

For $x = 1,500,\ y = 2(1,500) + 15000 = 3,000 + 15,000 = 18,000$

For $x = 2,000,\ y = 2(2,000) + 15000 = 4,000 + 15,000 = 19,000$

x	$C = 2x + 15000$	(x, y)
0	15000	(0, 15000)
500	16000	(500, 16000)
1000	17000	(1000, 17000)
1500	18000	(1500, 18000)
2000	19000	(2000, 19000)

x	$R = 12x$	(x, y)
0	0	(0, 0)
500	6000	(500, 6000)
1000	12000	(1000, 12000
1500	18000	(1500, 18000)
2000	20000	(2000, 24000)

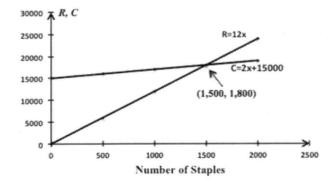

The break-even point is where the lines intersect: (1,500, 18,000).

5. (a) $\text{BEP} = x = \dfrac{F}{p-a} = \dfrac{\$15{,}000}{\$1.75-\$0.15} = \dfrac{\$15{,}000}{\$1.60} = 9{,}375$ bulbs

(b) $\text{BEP} = x = \dfrac{F}{p-a} = \dfrac{\$15{,}000}{\$2.50-\$0.15} = \dfrac{\$15{,}000}{\$2.35} = 6{,}383$ bulbs

(c) Yes, because if the selling price is higher, the manufacturer does not have to sell (produce) more bulbs.

7. We are to determine the variable cost, a, given BEP (or x) = 120, selling cost $p = 25$, and fixed cost $F = \$1{,}920$.

$\text{BEP} = x = \dfrac{F}{p-a}$

$120 = \dfrac{1{,}920}{25-a}$

$120(25-a) = \dfrac{1{,}920}{25-a}(25-a)$

$120(25-a) = \dfrac{1{,}920}{\cancel{25-a}}\cancel{(25-a)}$

$120(25-a) = 1{,}920$

$3{,}000 - 120a = 1{,}920$

$\begin{array}{cc} -3{,}000 & -3{,}000 \\ \hline -120a = -1{,}080 \end{array}$

$\dfrac{-120a}{-120} = \dfrac{-1{,}080}{-120}$

$a = 9$

The variable cost per bookend is $9.00.

Section 2.5: Quadratic Equations

1. If possible, rewrite equations (a) – (h) into the form $y = ax^2 + bx + c$.

(a) $x^2 - x = y$

$y = x^2 - x$

The given equation is a quadratic equation with x as the quadratic variable and $a = 1, b = -1$, and $c = 0$.

(b) $y^4 = 3$

$(y^4)^{1/4} = \pm 3^{1/4}$

$y = \pm\sqrt[4]{3}$

The given equation is not a quadratic equation, since it is not in the form: $y = ax^2 + bx + c$

(c) This equation is a quadratic equation with x as the quadratic variable and $a = 1$,

$b = -2, and\ c = 2.$

(d) Solve the equation for y. We have:

$$y - x^2 = 0$$
$$+ x^2 \quad\ + x^2$$
$$y = x^2$$

The given equation is a quadratic equation with x as the quadratic variable and $a = 1, b = 0,$ and $c = 0.$

(e) Solve the equation for y. We have: $y = -x + 3$. The given equation is not a quadratic equation since the exponent on x is not 2.

(f) Solve the given equation for d. We have:

$$2d + 5 = n^2$$
$$-5 \quad\ -5$$
$$2d = n^2 - 5$$

$$\frac{2d}{2} = \frac{n^2 - 5}{2}$$

$$d = \frac{n^2}{2} - \frac{5}{2}$$

The given equation is a quadratic equation with n as the quadratic variable and $a = \frac{1}{2}, b = 0,$ and $c = -\frac{5}{2}.$

(g) The given equation is a quadratic equation with S as the quadratic variable and $a = 2, b = 0,$ and $c = 0.$

(h) Solve the given equation for y. We have:

$$\left(y^{1/2}\right)^2 = x^2, \qquad x \geq 0\ and\ y \geq 0$$
$$y = x^2, \qquad\qquad x \geq 0\ and\ y \geq 0$$

The given equation is a quadratic equation with x as the quadratic variable with $a = 1, b = 0,$ and $c = 0.$

3. For (a) – (f), the solution(s) to $ax^2 + bx + c = 0$ is (are): $x = \dfrac{-b \pm \sqrt{b^2 - 4ac}}{2a}$.

(a) With $a = 1, b = -1,$ and $c = -6$, we have:

$$x = \frac{-b \pm \sqrt{b^2 - 4ac}}{2a} = \frac{-(-1) \pm \sqrt{(-1)^2 - 4(1)(-6)}}{2(1)} = \frac{1 \pm \sqrt{1 + 24}}{2} = \frac{1 \pm \sqrt{25}}{2} = \frac{1 \pm 5}{2}$$

$$x = \frac{1 + 5}{2} = \frac{6}{2} = 3 \ \ or \ \ x = \frac{1 - 5}{2} = \frac{-4}{2} = -2$$

(b) With $a = 3$, $b = -2$, and $c = -5$, we have:

$$x = \frac{-b \pm \sqrt{b^2 - 4ac}}{2a} = \frac{-(-2) \pm \sqrt{(-2)^2 - 4(3)(-5)}}{2(3)} = \frac{2 \pm \sqrt{4+60}}{6} = \frac{2 \pm \sqrt{64}}{6} = \frac{2 \pm 8}{6}$$

$$x = \frac{2+8}{6} = \frac{10}{6} = \frac{5}{3} \quad \text{or } x = \frac{2-8}{6} = \frac{-6}{6} = -1$$

(c) With $a = 4$, $b = 0$, and $c = -7$, we have:

$$x = \frac{-0 \pm \sqrt{(0)^2 - 4(4)(-7)}}{2(4)} = \frac{0 \pm \sqrt{0+112}}{8} = \frac{\pm\sqrt{112}}{8} = \frac{\pm\sqrt{16 \cdot 7}}{8} = \frac{\pm 4\sqrt{7}}{8} = \frac{\pm\sqrt{7}}{2}$$

$$x = \frac{\sqrt{7}}{2} \quad \text{or} \quad x = -\frac{\sqrt{7}}{2}$$

(d) Since $a = \frac{1}{3}$, we will remove the fraction in the equation by multiplying both sides by 3. We have:

$$3\left(\frac{1}{3}x^2 - x - 1\right) = 3 \cdot 0$$

$$3 \cdot \frac{1}{3}x^2 - 3x - 3 = 0$$

$$x^2 - 3x - 3 = 0$$

With, $a = 1$, $b = -3$, and $c = -3$, we have:

$$x = \frac{-b \pm \sqrt{b^2 - 4ac}}{2a} = \frac{-(-3) \pm \sqrt{(-3)^2 - 4(1)(-3)}}{2(1)} = \frac{3 \pm \sqrt{9+12}}{2} = \frac{3 \pm \sqrt{21}}{2}$$

$$x = \frac{3+\sqrt{21}}{2} \quad \text{or} \quad x = \frac{3-\sqrt{21}}{2}$$

(e) First, rewrite $x^2 - x = 4$ in the standard form: $ax^2 + bx + c = 0$. We have:

$$x^2 - x = 4$$
$$-4 \quad -4$$
$$x^2 - x - 4 = 0$$

With $a = 1$, $b = -1$, and $c = -4$, we have:

$$x = \frac{-b \pm \sqrt{b^2 - 4ac}}{2a} = \frac{-(-1) \pm \sqrt{(-1)^2 - 4(1)(-4)}}{2(1)} = \frac{1 \pm \sqrt{1+16}}{2} = \frac{1 \pm \sqrt{17}}{2}$$

$$x = \frac{1+\sqrt{17}}{2} \quad \text{or} \quad x = \frac{1-\sqrt{17}}{2}$$

(f) With $a = 3$, $b = -12$, and $c = 6$, we have:

$$x = \frac{-b \pm \sqrt{b^2 - 4ac}}{2a} = \frac{-(-12) \pm \sqrt{(-12)^2 - 4(3)(6)}}{2(3)} = \frac{12 \pm \sqrt{144 - 72}}{6}$$

$$= \frac{12 \pm \sqrt{72}}{6} = \frac{12 \pm \sqrt{36 \cdot 2}}{6} = \frac{12 \pm 6\sqrt{2}}{6} = \frac{6(2 \pm \sqrt{2})}{6} = 2 \pm \sqrt{2}$$

$$x = 2 + \sqrt{2} \quad \text{or} \quad x = 2 - \sqrt{2}$$

5. (a) $t = 3$ and $P = 25,000$

$$V = (-0.005 \cdot 3^2 - 0.05 \cdot 3 + 0.8)(25,000) = (-0.045 - 0.15 + 0.8)(25,000)$$
$$= 0.605(25,000) = \$15,125$$

(b) $t = 0$ and $P = 25,000$

$$V = \left(-0.005 \cdot 0^2 - 0.05 \cdot 0 + 0.8\right)(25,000) = (0 - 0 + 0.8)(25,000) = 0.8(25,000)$$
$$= \$20,000$$

(c) $V = 12,800$ and $P = 40,000$

$$12,800 = (-0.005t^2 - 0.05t + 0.8)(40,000)$$

$$(-0.005t^2 - 0.05t + .8)(40,000) = 12,800$$

$$-200t^2 - 2000t + 32,000 = 12,800$$

$$\underline{-12,800 \quad -12,800}$$

$$-200t^2 - 2,000t + 19,200 = 0$$

$$-200(t^2 + 10t - 96) = 0$$

$$\frac{-200(t^2 + 10t - 96)}{-200} = \frac{0}{-200}$$

$$t^2 + 10t - 96 = 0$$

Method 1: Solve by Factoring

$$(t + 16)(t - 6) = 0$$

$$t + 16 = 0 \qquad or \qquad t - 6 = 0$$
$$\underline{-16 \quad -16} \qquad\qquad \underline{+6 \quad +6}$$
$$t = -16 \qquad\qquad\qquad t = 6$$

Since time is positive, the only solution is $t = 6$ years.

Method 2: Use the Quadratic Formula

With $a = 1, b = 10, and\ c = -96$, we have:

$$t = \frac{-(10)\pm\sqrt{(10)^2-4(1)(-96)}}{2(1)} = \frac{-10\pm\sqrt{100+384}}{2}$$

$$= \frac{-10\pm\sqrt{484}}{2} = \frac{-10\pm22}{2}$$

$$t = \frac{-10+22}{2} = \frac{12}{2} = 6 \quad \text{or} \quad t = \frac{-10-22}{2} = \frac{-32}{2} = -16$$

Since time is positive, the only solution is $t = 6$ years.

Section 2.6: Polynomial Equations

1. (a) $y = x^5 - 2x^2$ represents a fifth-degree polynomial curve having the form

   $y = a_5x^5 + a_4x^4 + a_3x^3 + a_2x^2 + a_1x + a_0$, where $a_5 = 1, a_4 = 0, a_3 = 0,$
   $a_2 = -2, a_1 = 0, and\ a_0 = 0.$

   (b) Solving the equation for y, we have:

   $$(y^2)^{1/2} = \pm(x^3 + 1)^{1/2}$$

   $$y = \pm\sqrt{x^3 + 1}$$

   Therefore, the given equation does not represent a polynomial curve.

   (c) Solving the equation for y, we have:

   $$y - x^2 = x^4$$
   $$+ x^2 \quad + x^2$$
   $$y = x^4 + x^2$$

   Therefore, $y = x^4 + x^2$ represents a fourth-degree polynomial curve having the form

   $y = a_4x^4 + a_3x^3 + a_2x^2 + a_1x + a_0$, where $a_4 = 1, a_3 = 0, a_2 = 1, a_1 = 0$ and $a_0 = 0.$

   (d) Solving the equation for y, we have:

   $$(y^5)^{1/5} = 1^{1/5}$$

   $y = 1 = x^0.$ This is a constant polynomial of degree 0.

   (e) $y = x^2 - 2x + 5$ represents a second-degree polynomial(trinomial) curve having the f
   $y = a_2x^2 + a_1x + a_0$, where $a_2 = 1, a_1 = -2,$ and $a_0 = 5.$

(f) $y = \sqrt{x} + 1 = x^{1/2} + 1$ does not represent a polynomial curve, because the exponent on x is $\frac{1}{2}$, which is not a nonnegative integer.

Section 2.7: Exponential Equations

1. $y = 2(7^x)$ is an exponential equation with $a = 2$ and $b = 7$.

3. $y = 2(x^7)$ is not an exponential equation because the base is x and not a fixed nonnegative number.

5. Using the Power Rule for exponents, we can rewrite the equation $y = (7^x)^2$ to $y = 7^{2x}$. Applying the Product Rule to $y = 7^{2x}$, we can rewrite it to $y = (7^2)^x = 49^x$. Therefore, $y = 7^{2x}$ is an exponential equation with $a = 1$ and $b = 49$.

7. $y = 2\left(-\frac{1}{2}\right)^x$ is not an exponential equation because the base $b = -\frac{1}{2}$ is negative.

9. $y = 9(1.1)^x$ is an exponential equation with $a = 9$ and $b = 1.1$.

11. (a) *Number of Bacteria* $= 100e^{0.2(10)} = 100(7.3891) = 739$ bacteria.

(b) *Number of Bacteria* $= 100e^{0.2(24)} = 100(121.5104) = 12{,}151$ bacteria.

(c) *Number of Bacteria* $= 100e^{0.2(36)} = 100(1{,}339.4308) = 133{,}943$ bacteria.

(d) *Number of Bacteria* $= 100e^{0.2(48)} = 100(14{,}764.7816) = 1{,}476{,}478$ bacteria.

13. (a) *Remaining Material* $= 100e^{-0.00012(1{,}000)} = 100(0.8869) = 88.69$ grams.

(b) *Remaining Material* $= 250e^{-0.00012(500)} = 250(0.9418) = 235.45$ grams.

Chapter 3: The Mathematics of Finance

Section 3.1: Compound Interest

1. (a) $i = \frac{r}{1} = \frac{0.02}{1} = 0.02, \ n = 1(4) = 4, P(0) = \$2,000$

   (b) $P(n) = (1 + i)^n P(0) = P(0)(1 + i)^n$

   $P(4) = P(4) = \$2,000(1 + .02)^4 = \$2,000(1.02)^4 = \$2,164.86$

3. $i = \frac{r}{1} = \frac{0.04}{1} = 0.04, \ n = 1(3) = 3, P(0) = \$2,500$

   $P(n) = (1 + i)^n P(0) = P(0)(1 + i)^n$

   $P(3) = P(3) = \$2,500(1 + .04)^3 = \$2,500(1.04)^3 = \$2,812.16$

5. $i = \frac{r}{4} = \frac{0.05}{4} = 0.0125, n = 4(3) = 12, P(0) = \$2,500$

   $P(n) = (1 + i)^n P(0) = P(0)(1 + i)^n$

   $P(12) = \$2,500(1 + 0.0125)^{12} = \$2,500(1.0125)^{12} = \$2,901.89$

7. $i = \frac{r}{1} = \frac{0.025}{1} = 0.025, n = 1(25) = 25, \ P(0) = \$1,000$

   $P(n) = (1 + i)^n P(0) = P(0)(1 + i)^n$

   $P(25) = \$1,000(1 + .025)^{25} = \$1,000(1.025)^{25} = \$1,853.94$

9. $i = \frac{r}{12} = \frac{0.015}{12} = 0.00125, n = 3(12) = 36, P(0) = \$2,900$

   $P(n) = (1 + i)^n P(0) = P(0)(1 + i)^n$

   $P(36) = \$2,900(1 + .00125)^{36} = \$2,900(1.00125)^{36} = \$3,033.40$

11. $i = \frac{r}{365} = \frac{0.025}{365}, n = 365(4) = 1,460, P(0) = \$3,500$

   $P(n) = (1 + i)^n P(0) = P(0)(1 + i)^n$

   $P(1,460) = \$3,500 \left(1 + \frac{.025}{365}\right)^{1,460} = \$3,868.08$

13. $i = \frac{r}{365} = \frac{0.03}{365}, n = 365(3) = 1,095, P(0) = \$2,500$

   $P(n) = (1 + i)^n P(0) = P(0)(1 + i)^n$

   $P(1,095) = \$2,500 \left(1 + \frac{.03}{356}\right)^{1,095} = \$2,735.43$

Section 3.2: Comparing Investment Alternatives

1. (a) $FV = P(0)(1+i)^n = P(0)\left(1+\frac{r}{1}\right)^n = \$5,000\left(1+\frac{0.04}{1}\right)^{1\cdot 10}$

$= \$5,000(1.04)^{10} = \$7,401.22$

(b) $FV = P(0)(1+i)^n = P(0)\left(1+\frac{r}{2}\right)^n = \$5,000\left(1+\frac{0.04}{2}\right)^{2\cdot 10}$

$= \$5,000(1.02)^{20} = \$7,429.74$

(c) $FV = P(0)(1+i)^n = P(0)\left(1+\frac{r}{4}\right)^n = \$5,000\left(1+\frac{0.04}{4}\right)^{4\cdot 10}$

$= \$5,000(1.01)^{40} = \$7,444.32$

(d) $FV = P(0)(1+i)^n = P(0)\left(1+\frac{r}{365}\right)^n = \$5,000\left(1+\frac{0.04}{365}\right)^{365\cdot 10}$

$= \$5,000\left(1+\frac{0.04}{365}\right)^{3650} = \$7,458.96$

3. $FV = P(0)(1+i)^n = P(0)\left(1+\frac{r}{4}\right)^n = \$12,000\left(1+\frac{0.05}{4}\right)^{4\cdot 7}$

$= \$12,000(1+.0125)^{28} = \$12,000(1.0125)^{28} = \$16,991.91$

5. **At 2%:** $FV = P(0)(1+i)^n = P(0)\left(1+\frac{r}{4}\right)^n = \$2,000\left(1+\frac{0.015}{4}\right)^{4\cdot 1}$

$= \$1,000(1.005)^4 = \$1,020.15$

At 4%: $FV = P(0)(1+i)^n = P(0)\left(1+\frac{r}{1}\right)^n = \$1,000\left(1+\frac{.04}{1}\right)^1$

$= \$1,000(1.04) = \$1,040$

Therefore, *assuming equal credit risk for both alternative*, the 4% annually is the better investment alternative.

7. Time savings plan: $FV = P(0)(1+i)^n = P(0)\left(1+\frac{r}{1}\right)^n = \$2,000\left(1+\frac{0.015}{1}\right)^{3\cdot 1}$

$= \$2,091.36$

Loan to friend: FV = \$750(3) = \$2,250

Therefore, *assuming equal credit risk for both alternative*, lending to your friend is the better investment alternative.

9. (a) $PV = (1+i)^{-n}FV = FV(1+i)^{-n} = FV\left(1+\frac{r}{1}\right)^{-n} = \$15,000\left(1+\frac{0.02}{1}\right)^{-8\cdot 1}$

$= \$12,802.36$

(b) $PV = FV(1+i)^{-n} = FV\left(1+\frac{r}{1}\right)^{-n} = \$15,000\left(1+\frac{0.04}{1}\right)^{-8\cdot1}$

$\quad = \$15,000(1+.04)^{-8} = \$10,960.35$

(c) $PV = FV(1+i)^{-n} = FV\left(1+\frac{r}{1}\right)^{-n} = \$15,000\left(1+\frac{.08}{1}\right)^{-8\cdot1}$

$\quad = \$15,000(1.08)^{-8} = \$8,104.03$

(d) The Present Value of a Future Value amount goes down (that is, decreases) as the interest rate increases.

11. $PV = FV(1+i)^{-n} = FV\left(1+\frac{r}{2}\right)^{-n} = \$10,000\left(1+\frac{0.04}{2}\right)^{-4.5(2)} = \$10,000(1.02)^{-9}$

$\quad = \$8,367.55$

13. Calculate the future value of \$10,000 invested at 4% for 3 years compounding quarterly.

$\quad FV = P(0)(1+i)^n = P(0)\left(1+\frac{r}{4}\right)^n = \$10,000\left(1+\frac{0.04}{4}\right)^{4\cdot3} = \$10,000(1.01)^{12}$

$\quad = \$11,268.25.$

In a friend's business she will receive \$12,000 in three years. Investing at 4% account yield \$11,268.25. Therefore, ***assuming equal credit risk for both alternative***, she gets a better return from her friend's business.

15. Find the Present Value for each Buyer.

Buyer A:

$PV_A = FV(1+i)^{-n} = FV\left(1+\frac{r}{1}\right)^{-n} = \$5,000\left(1+\frac{0.04}{1}\right)^{-1\cdot4} = \$5,000(1.04)^{-4}$
$\quad = \$4,274.02$

Total Present value $= \$20,000 + PV_A = \$20,000 + \$4,274.02 = \$24,274.02$

Buyer B:

$PV_B = FV(1+i)^{-n} = FV\left(1+\frac{r}{1}\right)^{-n} = \$10,000\left(1+\frac{0.04}{1}\right)^{-1\cdot3} = \$10,000(1.04)^{-3}$
$\quad = \$8,889.96$

Total Present value $= \$15,000 + PV_B = \$15,000 + \$8,889.96 = \$23,889.96$

Buyer C:

$PV_C = FV(1+i)^{-n} = FV\left(1+\frac{r}{1}\right)^{-n} = \$18,000\left(1+\frac{0.04}{1}\right)^{-1\cdot6} = \$18,000(1.04)^{-6}$
$\quad = \$14,225.66$

Total Present value $= \$10,000 + PV_C = \$10,000 + \$14,225.66 = \$24,225.66$

Assuming equal credit risk, Buyer A has made the best offer with \$24,270.02.

17. **1st Opportunity**:

$$PV = FV(1+i)^{-n} = FV\left(1+\frac{r}{1}\right)^{-n} = \$8,000\left(1+\frac{0.06}{1}\right)^{-1\cdot 4} = \$8,000(1.06)^{-4}$$
$$= \$6,336.75$$

2nd Opportunity:

$$PV = FV(1+i)^{-n} = FV\left(1+\frac{r}{1}\right)^{-n} = \$7,000\left(1+\frac{0.06}{1}\right)^{-1\cdot 2} = \$7,000(1.06)^{-2}$$
$$= \$6,229.98$$

3rd Opportunity:

$$PV = FV(1+i)^{-n} = FV\left(1+\frac{r}{1}\right)^{-n} = \$10,000\left(1+\frac{.06}{1}\right)^{-1\cdot 7} = \$10,000(1.06)^{-7}$$
$$= \$6,650.57$$

Assuming equal credit risk, the 3rd opportunity is best.

19. $i = \left(\frac{FV}{PV}\right)^{1/n} - 1 = \left(\frac{1,350}{1,000}\right)^{\frac{1}{3}} - 1 = 1.1052 - 1 = .1052 = 10.52\%$

21. $i = \left(\frac{2x}{x}\right)^{1/10} - 1 = (2)^{0.10} - 1 = 1.0718 - 1 = 0.0718 = 7.18\%$

Section 3.3: Net Present Values of Cash Flows

1. $PV_1 = FV(1+i)^{-n} = FV\left(1+\frac{r}{1}\right)^{-n} = \$750\left(1+\frac{0.02}{1}\right)^{-1\cdot 1} = \$750(1.02)^{-1}$
$$= \$735.29$$

$PV_2 = FV(1+i)^{-n} = FV\left(1+\frac{r}{1}\right)^{-n} = \$1,100\left(1+\frac{0.02}{1}\right)^{-1\cdot 2} = \$1,100(1.02)^{-2}$
$$= \$1,057.29$$

$PV_3 = FV(1+i)^{-n} = FV\left(1+\frac{r}{1}\right)^{-n} = \$2,000\left(1+\frac{0.02}{1}\right)^{-1\cdot 4} = \$2,000(1.02)^{-4}$
$$= \$1,847.69$$

$NPV = (PV_1 + PV_2 + PV_3) - C_0 = \$3,640.27 - \$2,500 = \$1,140.27$

Yes. This is a profitable investment.

3. $PV_1 = FV(1+i)^{-n} = FV\left(1+\frac{r}{12}\right)^{-n} = \$500\left(1+\frac{0.025}{12}\right)^{-0.5(12)}$
$$= \$500\left(1+\frac{0.025}{12}\right)^{-6} = \$493.80$$

$$PV_2 = FV(1+i)^{-n} = FV\left(1+\frac{r}{12}\right)^{-n} = \$1,000\left(1+\frac{.025}{12}\right)^{-1.25(12)}$$

$$= \$1,000\left(1+\frac{0.025}{12}\right)^{-15} = \$969.26$$

$$PV_3 = FV(1+i)^{-n} = FV\left(1+\frac{r}{12}\right)^{-n} = \$2,000\left(1+\frac{0.025}{12}\right)^{-3(12)}$$

$$= \$2,000\left(1+\frac{0.025}{12}\right)^{-36} = \$1,855.63$$

Total Present Value $= PV_1 + PV_2 + PV_3 = \$3,318.69$

Net Present Value $= NPV = \$3,318.69 - \$2,900 = \$418.69$

Section 3.4: Ordinary Annuities

1. $PV = R\left[\frac{1-(1+i)^{-n}}{i}\right] = \$50\left[\frac{1-\left(1+\frac{0.04}{4}\right)^{-4\cdot10}}{\frac{0.04}{4}}\right] = \$50\left[\frac{1-(1.01)^{-40}}{.01}\right] = \$1,641.73$

3. $PV = R\left[\frac{1-(1+i)^{-n}}{i}\right] = \$750\left[\frac{1-\left(1+\frac{0.08}{1}\right)^{-1\cdot3}}{\frac{0.08}{1}}\right] = \$750\left[\frac{1-(1.08)^{-3}}{.08}\right] = \$1,932.82$

$NPV = PV - C_0 = \$1,932.82 - \$1,500 = \$432.82$

5. **1st Investment**:

$$PV_1 = R\left[\frac{1-(1+i)^{-n}}{i}\right] = \$2,000\left[\frac{1-\left(1+\frac{0.04}{12}\right)^{-12\cdot2}}{\frac{0.04}{12}}\right] = \$2,000\left[\frac{1-\left(1+\frac{0.04}{12}\right)^{-24}}{\frac{0.04}{12}}\right]$$

$$= \$2,000\left(\frac{12}{0.04}\right)\left[1-\left(1+\frac{0.04}{12}\right)^{-24}\right] = \$46,056.50$$

$$PV_2 = FV(1+i)^{-n} = \$38,000\left(1+\frac{0.04}{12}\right)^{-12\cdot2} = \$38,000\left(1+\frac{0.04}{12}\right)^{-24}$$

$$= \$35,083.09$$

$$NPV_1 = PV_1 + PV_2 - C_0 = \$46,056.50 + \$35,083.09 - \$70,000$$

$$= \$11,139.59$$

2ⁿᵈ Investment:

$$PV = R\left[\frac{1-(1+i)^{-n}}{i}\right] = \$3{,}500\left[\frac{1-\left(1+\frac{0.04}{12}\right)^{-12\cdot2}}{\frac{0.04}{12}}\right] = \$3{,}500\left[\frac{1-\left(1+\frac{0.04}{12}\right)^{-24}}{\frac{0.04}{12}}\right]$$

$$= \$3{,}500\left(\frac{12}{0.04}\right)\left[1-\left(1+\frac{0.04}{12}\right)^{-24}\right] = \$80{,}598.88$$

$$NPV_2 = PV - C_0 = \$80{,}598.88 - \$70{,}000 = \$10{,}598.88$$

On a strictly monetary basis, and assuming equal credit risk for both investments, the first investment is more profitable.

7. **1ˢᵗ Investment:**

$$PV = R\left[\frac{1-(1+i)^{-n}}{i}\right] = \$2{,}300\left[\frac{1-\left(1+\frac{0.04}{4}\right)^{-4\cdot3}}{\frac{0.04}{4}}\right] = \$2{,}300\left[\frac{1-(1+0.01)^{-12}}{0.01}\right]$$

$$= \$25{,}886.68$$

$$NPV_1 = PV - C_0 = \$25{,}886.68 - \$20{,}000 = \$5{,}886.68$$

2ⁿᵈ Investment:

$$PV = R\left[\frac{1-(1+i)^{-n}}{i}\right] = \$1{,}500\left[\frac{1-\left(1+\frac{0.04}{4}\right)^{-4\cdot4}}{\frac{0.04}{4}}\right] = \$1{,}500\left[\frac{1-(1+0.01)^{-16}}{0.01}\right]$$

$$= \$22{,}076.81$$

$$NPV_2 = PV + 2{,}000 - C_0 = \$22{,}076.81 + \$2{,}000 - \$18{,}000$$

On a strictly monetary basis, and assuming equal credit risk for both i[...] second investment is more profitable. (Note: to compare investments t[...] must be considered in both NPVs. Thus, in the second alternative, after [...] there is still $2,000 of intermediate, or Present Value, funds available, w[...] added to the NPV.)

9. $$PV_1 = R\left[\frac{1-(1+i)^{-n}}{i}\right] = \$80\left[\frac{1-\left(1+\frac{0.06}{2}\right)^{-20}}{\frac{0.06}{2}}\right] = \$80\left[\frac{1-(1+0.03)^{-20}}{0.03}\right] = \$1{,}190.20$$

$$PV_2 = \$1{,}000\left(1+\frac{0.06}{2}\right)^{-20} = \$1{,}000(1+0.03)^{-20} = \$553.68$$

Total Present value $= PV_1 + PV_2 = \$1{,}190.20 + \$553.68 = \$1{,}743.88$

11. $FV = R\left[\dfrac{(1+i)^n-1}{i}\right] = \$40\left[\dfrac{\left(1+\frac{0.04}{4}\right)^{4\cdot 3}-1}{\frac{0.04}{4}}\right] = \$400\left[\dfrac{(1+0.01)^{12}-1}{0.01}\right]$

$\quad\quad = \$400\left[\dfrac{(1.01)^{12}-1}{.01}\right] = \$5{,}073.00$

13. $FV = R\left[\dfrac{(1+i)^n-1}{i}\right] = \$20\left[\dfrac{\left(1+\frac{0.05}{52}\right)^{52\cdot\frac{48}{52}}-1}{\frac{0.05}{52}}\right]$

$\quad\quad = \$20\left(\dfrac{52}{0.05}\right)\left[\left(1+\dfrac{0.05}{52}\right)^{48}-1\right] = \$982.02$

Section 3.5: Mortgages and Amortization Tables

1. $R = \dfrac{PV}{\left[\dfrac{1-(1+i)^{-n}}{i}\right]} = \dfrac{\$36{,}000}{\left[\dfrac{1-\left(1+\frac{0.04}{12}\right)^{-30\cdot 12}}{\frac{0.04}{12}}\right]} = \dfrac{\$36{,}000}{\left[\dfrac{1-\left(1+\frac{0.04}{12}\right)^{-360}}{\frac{0.04}{12}}\right]} = \dfrac{\$36{,}000}{\left[\dfrac{.6982041}{\frac{0.04}{12}}\right]}$

$\quad\quad = \dfrac{\$36{,}000}{209.4612404} = \$171.87$

3. Total Interest Paid $= (R\cdot n) - PV = (\$171.87\cdot 12\cdot 30) - \$36{,}000$

$\quad\quad = \$61{,}873.20 - \$36{,}000 = \$25{,}873.20$

5. **See Figure 3.9 Column D in the textbook**

Total Interest Paid

$= \$4.17 + \$3.83 + \$3.49 + \$3.14 + \$2.80 + \$2.46 + \$2.11 + \$1.76 + \$1.41 + \$1.06 + \$0.71 + \$0.36$
$= \$27.30$

See Equation 3.17 in the textbook

Total Interest Paid $= (R\cdot n) - PV = (\$85.61\cdot 1\cdot 12) - \$1{,}000 = \$27.32^*$

* The two answers are slightly different due to rounding.

7. (a) $R = \dfrac{PV}{\left[\dfrac{1-(1+i)^{-n}}{i}\right]} = \dfrac{\$45{,}000}{\left[\dfrac{1-\left(1+\frac{0.04}{12}\right)^{-4\cdot12}}{\frac{0.04}{12}}\right]} = \dfrac{\$45{,}000}{\left[\dfrac{1-\left(1+\frac{0.04}{12}\right)^{-48}}{\frac{0.04}{12}}\right]} = \dfrac{\$45{,}000}{\left[\dfrac{0.1476294}{\frac{0.04}{12}}\right]}$

$= \dfrac{\$45{,}000}{44.28882} = \$1{,}016.06$

(b) Total Interest Paid $= (R \cdot n) - PV = (\$1{,}016.06 \cdot 12 \cdot 4) - \$45{,}000$

$= \$48{,}770.88 - \$45{,}000 = \$3{,}770.88$

(c) **Payment 1**:

Interest Paid $= I_1 = (\$45{,}000)\left(\frac{0.04}{12}\right) = \$150$

Principal Paid $= Monthly\ Payment - Interest\ Paid = \$1{,}016.06 - \$150 = \$866.06$

Outstanding Balance $= \$45{,}000 - Principal\ Paid = \$45{,}000 - \$866.06 = \$44{,}133.94$

Payment 2:

Interest Paid $= I_2 = (\$44{,}133.94)\left(\frac{0.04}{12}\right) = \$147.11$

Principal Paid $= Monthly\ Payment - Interest\ Paid = \$1{,}016.06 - \$147.11 = \$868.95$

Outstanding Balance $= \$45{,}000 - Principal\ Paid = \$44{,}133.94 - \$868.95 = \$43{,}264.99$

Payment 3:

Interest Paid $= I_3 = (\$43{,}264.99)\left(\frac{0.04}{12}\right) = \$144.22$

Principal Paid $= Monthly\ Payment - Interest\ Paid = \$1{,}016.06 - \$144.2 = \$871.84$

Outstanding Balance $= \$43{,}264.99 - Principal\ Paid = \$43{,}264.99 - \$871.84 = \$42{,}393.15$

	A	B	C	D	E	F	G
1	Amount of Loan:	$45,000					
2	Length of Loan (in years):	4					
3	Annual Interest Rate:	4%					
4	Monthly Payment:	$1,016.06					
5							
6			Payment Number	Payment Amount	Interest Paid	Principal Paid	Outstanding Balance
7			0	-	-	-	$45,000.00
8			1	$1,016.06	$150.00	$866.06	$44,133.94
9			2	$1,016.06	$147.11	$868.95	$43,264.99
10			3	$1,016.06	$144.22	$871.84	$42,393.15

9. Monthly Payment:

$$R = \frac{PV}{\left[\frac{1-(1+i)^{-n}}{i}\right]} = \frac{\$800}{\left[\frac{1-\left(1+\frac{0.04}{12}\right)^{-1\cdot12}}{\frac{0.04}{12}}\right]} = \frac{\$800}{\left[\frac{1-\left(1+\frac{0.04}{12}\right)^{-12}}{\frac{0.04}{12}}\right]} = \frac{\$800}{\left[\frac{.039146648}{\frac{0.04}{12}}\right]}$$

$$= \frac{\$800}{11.7439944} = \$68.12$$

Payment 1:

Interest Paid $= I_1 = (\$800)\left(\frac{0.04}{12}\right) = \$2.67$

Principal Paid $= Monthly\ Payment - Interest\ Paid = \$68.12 - \$2.67 = \$65.45$

Outstanding Balance $= \$800 - Principal\ Paid = \$800 - \$65.45 = \$734.55$

Payment 2:

Interest Paid $= I_2 = (\$734.55)\left(\frac{0.04}{12}\right) = \$2.45$

Principal Paid $= Monthly\ Payment - Interest\ Paid = \$68.12 - \$2.45 = \$65.67$

Outstanding Balance $= \$734.55 - Principal\ Paid = \$734.55 - \$65.67 = \$668.88$

Payment 3:

Interest Paid $= I_3 = (\$668.88)\left(\frac{0.04}{12}\right) = \$2.23$

Principal Paid $= Monthly\ Payment - Interest\ Paid = \$68.12 - \$2.23 = \$65.89$

Outstanding Balance $= \$668.88 - Principal\ Paid = \$668.88 - \$65.89 = \$602.99$

Payment 4:

Interest Paid $= I_4 = (\$602.99)\left(\frac{0.04}{12}\right) = \$2.01$

Principal Paid $= Monthly\ Payment - Interest\ Paid = \$68.12 - \$2.01 = \$66.11$

Outstanding Balance $= \$602.99 - Principal\ Paid = \$602.99 - \$66.11 = \$536.88$

Payment 5:

Interest Paid $= I_5 = (\$536.88)\left(\frac{0.04}{12}\right) = \$1.79$

Principal Paid $= Monthly\ Payment - Interest\ Paid = \$68.12 - \$1.79 = \$66.33$

Outstanding Balance $= \$536.88 - Principal\ Paid = \$536.88 - \$66.33 = \$470.55$

Payment 6:

Interest Paid $= I_6 = (\$470.55)\left(\frac{0.04}{12}\right) = \$1.57$

Principal Paid $= Monthly\ Payment - Interest\ Paid = \$68.12 - \$1.57 = \$66.55$

Outstanding Balance $= \$470.55 - Principal\ Paid = \$470.55 - \$66.55 = \$404.00$

Payment 7:

Interest Paid $= I_7 = (\$404)\left(\frac{0.04}{12}\right) = \$1.35$

Principal Paid $= Monthly\ Payment - Interest\ Paid = \$68.12 - \$1.35 = \$66.77$

Outstanding Balance $= \$404 - Principal\ Paid = \$404 - \$66.77 = \$337.23$

Payment 8:

Interest Paid $= I_8 = (\$337.23)\left(\frac{0.04}{12}\right) = \$1.12$

Principal Paid $= Monthly\ Payment - Interest\ Paid = \$68.12 - \$1.12 = \$67.00$

Outstanding Balance $= \$337.23 - Principal\ Paid = \$337.23 - \$67.00 = \$270.23$

Payment 9:

Interest Paid $= I_9 = (\$270.23)\left(\frac{0.04}{12}\right) = \$0.90$

Principal Paid $= Monthly\ Payment - Interest\ Paid = \$68.12 - \$0.90 = \$67.22$

Outstanding Balance $= \$270.23 - Principal\ Paid = \$270.23 - \$67.22 = \$203.01$

Payment 10:

Interest Paid $= I_{10} = (\$203.01)\left(\frac{0.04}{12}\right) = \$0.68$

Principal Paid $= Monthly\ Payment - Interest\ Paid = \$68.12 - \$0.68 = \$67.44$

Outstanding Balance $= \$203.01 - Principal\ Paid = \$203.01 - \$67.44 = \$135.57$

Payment 11:

Interest Paid $= I_{11} = (\$135.57)\left(\frac{0.04}{12}\right) = \$0.45$

Principal Paid $= Monthly\ Payment - Interest\ Paid = \$68.12 - \$0.45 = \$67.67$

Outstanding Balance $= \$135.57 - Principal\ Paid = \$135.57 - \$67.67 = \$67.90$

Payment 12:

Interest Paid $= I_{12} = (\$67.90)\left(\frac{0.04}{12}\right) = \$0.23$

Principal Paid $= Monthly\ Payment - Interest\ Paid = \$68.12 - \$0.23 = \$67.89$.

* Because of rounding, the last payment should be \$67.90 instead of 67.89 as calculated.

Outstanding Balance $= 0$

	A	B	C	D	E	F	G
1	Amount of Loan:	$800					
2	Length of Loan (in years):	1					
3	Annual Interest Rate:	4%					
4	Monthly Payment:	$68.12					
5							
6			Payment Number	Payment Amount	Interest Paid	Principal Paid	Outstanding Balance
7			0	-	-	-	$800.00
8			1	$68.12	$2.67	$65.45	$734.55
9			2	$68.12	$2.45	$65.67	$668.88
10			3	$68.12	$2.23	$65.89	$602.99
11			4	$68.12	$2.01	$66.11	$536.88
12			5	$68.12	$1.79	$66.33	$470.55
13			6	$68.12	$1.57	$66.55	$404.00
14			7	$68.12	$1.35	$66.77	$337.23
15			8	$68.12	$1.12	$67.00	$270.23
16			9	$68.12	$0.90	$67.22	$203.01
17			10	$68.12	$0.68	$67.44	$135.57
18			11	$68.12	$0.45	$67.67	$67.90
19			12	$68.12	$0.23	$67.90	$0.00

Section 3.6: Installment Loans and Interest Charges

1. (a) Total Interest Charge $= (0.08)(\$3,000)(2) = \$480$

   Monthly installment payment $= \dfrac{\$480 + \$3,000}{12(2)} = \dfrac{\$3,480}{24} = \$145.00$

   (b) Total Interest Charge $= (0.08)(\$3,000)(3) = \$720.00$

   Monthly installment payment $= \dfrac{\$720 + \$3,000}{12(3)} = \dfrac{\$3,720}{36} = \$103.33$

   (c) 14.677% for the 2 year loan; 14.546% for the 3 year loan.

3. (a) Total Interest Charge $= (0.06)(\$4,000)(1) = \$240$

   (b) Monthly installment payment $= \dfrac{\$240 + \$4,000}{12(1)} = \dfrac{\$4,240}{12} = \$353.33$

   (c) For Present Value of $4,000, a payment of $353.33 for 12 months (1 year), the true interest rate is 10.895%.

5. (a) Monthly payment $= \dfrac{\$9,000}{12(3)} = \dfrac{\$9,000}{36} = \$250$

   (b) Total Interest Charge $= (0.06)(\$9,000)(3) = \$1,620.00$

   (c) Cash Received = Amount of loan – Total interest charge $= \$9,000 - \$1,620 = \$7,380$

   (d) For a Present Value of $7,380, a payment of $250 for 36 months, the true interest is 13.376%.

7. (a) $Amount\ of\ loan = \dfrac{cash\ Received}{1-rt} = \dfrac{\$15,000}{1-(0.04)(5)} = \dfrac{\$15,000}{0.8} = \$18,750$

   (b) $R = \dfrac{Amount\ of\ Loan}{Length\ of\ loan, in\ months} = \dfrac{\$18,750}{12(5)} = \dfrac{\$18,750}{60} = \$312.50$

   (c) Total interest charge $= \$18,750 - \$15,000 = \$3,750$

   (d) For a Present Value of $15,000, a payment of $312.50 for 60 months (5 years), the true interest rate is 9.154%.

Section 3.7: Annuities Due

1. $PV = R + R\left[\dfrac{1-(1+i)^{-(n-1)}}{i}\right] = \$1,000 + \$1,000\left[\dfrac{1-\left(1+\frac{0.04}{1}\right)^{-(10\cdot 1-1)}}{\frac{0.04}{1}}\right]$

$= \$1,000 + \$1,000\left[\dfrac{1-(1+0.04)^{-9}}{0.04}\right] = \$1,000 + \$1,000(7.435332)$

$= \$1,000 + \$7,435.33 = \$8,435.33$

3. $PV = R + R\left[\dfrac{1-(1+i)^{-(n-1)}}{i}\right] = \$20 + \$20\left[\dfrac{1-\left(1+\frac{0.02}{12}\right)^{-(15\cdot 12-1)}}{\frac{0.02}{12}}\right]$

$$= \$20 + \$20 \left[\frac{1-\left(1+\frac{0.02}{12}\right)^{-179}}{\frac{0.02}{12}} \right] = \$20 + \$20 \left[\frac{0.2577618}{0.0016667} \right]$$

$$= \$20 + \$20(154.6539869) = \$20 + \$3{,}093.08 = \$3{,}113.08$$

5. $FV = R\left[\frac{(1+i)^{(n+1)}-1}{i}\right] - R = \$40\left[\frac{\left(1+\frac{0.04}{4}\right)^{(4\cdot3+1)}-1}{\frac{0.04}{4}}\right] - \$40$

$$= \$40\left[\frac{(1+0.01)^{13}-1}{0.01}\right] - \$40 = \$40(13.8093280) - \$40$$

$$= \$552.37 - \$40 = \$512.37$$

7. $FV = R\left[\frac{(1+i)^{(n+1)}-1}{i}\right] - R = \$20\left[\frac{\left(1+\frac{0.05}{52}\right)^{\left(52\cdot\frac{48}{52}+1\right)}-1}{\frac{0.05}{52}}\right] - \$20$

$$= \$20\left[\frac{\left(1+\frac{.05}{52}\right)^{(48+1)}}{\frac{.05}{52}}\right] - \$20 = \$20\left[\frac{\left(1+\frac{.05}{52}\right)^{49}-1}{\frac{.05}{52}}\right] - \$20$$

$$= \$20\left[\frac{0.0482192}{0.0009615}\right] - \$20 = \$20(50.149974) - \$20$$

$$= \$1{,}003 - \$20 = \$983.00$$

9. $FV = R\left[\frac{(1+i)^{(n+1)}-1}{i}\right] - R = \$1\left[\frac{\left(1+\frac{0.05}{365}\right)^{(365\cdot2+1)}-1}{\frac{0.05}{365}}\right] - \$1$

$$= \$1\left[\frac{\left(1+\frac{0.05}{365}\right)^{731}-1}{\frac{0.05}{365}}\right] - \$1 = \$1\left[\frac{0.1053147}{0.000137}\right] - \$1 = \$1(768.72) - \$1$$

$$= \$768.72 - \$1 = \$767.72$$

11. $FV = R\left[\frac{(1+i)^{(n+1)}-1}{i}\right] - R = \$1{,}000\left[\frac{\left(1+\frac{0.08}{1}\right)^{(1\cdot7+1)}-1}{\frac{0.08}{1}}\right] - \$1{,}000$

$$= \$1{,}000\left[\frac{(1.08)^{8}-1}{0.08}\right] - \$1{,}000 = \$1{,}000(10.636628) - \$1{,}000$$

$$= \$10{,}636.63 - \$1{,}000 = \$9{,}636.63$$

Section 3.8: Effective Interest Rate

1. $E = (1 + i)^n - 1 = \left(1 + \frac{0.02}{4}\right)^4 - 1 = (1.005)^4 - 1 = 0.020151 = 2.0151\%$

3. $E_c = e^i - 1 = e^{0.02} - 1 = 0.020201 = 2.0201\%$

5. $E_c = e^i - 1 = e^{0.04} - 1 = 0.040811 = 4.0811\%$

7. $E = (1 + i)^n - 1 = \left(1 + \frac{0.08}{4}\right)^4 - 1 = (1.02)^4 - 1 = 0.0824322 = 8.2432\%$

Chapter 4 Rates of Change: The Derivative

Section 4.1: Concept of a Function

1. The relation defines a function, because each element in the first set is assigned to only one element in the second set.

3. The relation does not define a function, because the element *a* in the first set is assigned to two elements, *A* and *B*, in the second set.

5. The relation defines a function, because each element in the first set is assigned to only one element in the second set.

7. The relation does not define a function, because the element *b* in the first set is is not assigned to any element in the second set.

9. The relation defines a function, because each element in the first set is assigned to only one element in the second set.

11. The relation defines a function, because each element in the first set is assigned to only one element in the second set.

13. The relation defines a function, because each element in the first set is assigned to only one element in the second set. No *x* component repeats.

15. (a) The relation defines a function, because each student has only one height measurement.

   (b) The relation defines a function, because each student has only one name.

   (c) The relation does not define a function, because a name could belong to more than one student.

   (d) The relation defines a function, because each stock that is listed on the New York Exchange has only one closing price.

   (e) The relation does not define a function, because a closing stock price might be the same for more than one stock listed on the New York Stock Exchange.

   (f) The relation does not define a function, because each car might have more than one color painted on it.

   (g) The relation does not define a function, because the same rate might be offered at more than bank.

Section 4.2: Mathematical Functions

1. (a) Domain = {0, 1, 2, 3, 4, 5, 6, 7, 8, 9, 10}

   (b) integers

   (c) To find the range of the function, evaluate the function at each z-value in Part (a). We have:

   For $z = 0, D = (0)^2 - 30(0) + 225 = 225$

   For $z = 1, D = (1)^2 - 30(1) + 225 = 196$

   For $z = 2, D = (2)^2 - 30(2) + 225 = 4 - 60 + 225 = 169$

   For $z = 3, D = (3)^2 - 30(3) + 225 = 9 - 90 + 225 = 144$

   For $z = 4, D = (4)^2 - 30(4) + 225 = 16 - 120 + 225 = 121$

   For $z = 5, D = (5)^2 - 30(5) + 225 = 25 - 150 + 225 = 100$

   For $z = 6, D = (6)^2 - 30(6) + 225 = 36 - 180 + 225 = 81$

   For $z = 7, D = (7)^2 - 30(7) + 225 = 49 - 210 + 225 = 64$

   For $z = 8, D = (8)^2 - 30(8) + 225 = 64 - 240 + 225 = 49$

   For $z = 9, D = (9)^2 - 30(9) + 225 = 81 - 270 + 225 = 36$

   For $z = 10, D = (10)^2 - 30(10) + 225 = 100 - 300 + 225 = 25$

   Range = {225, 196, 169, 144, 121, 100, 81, 64, 49, 36, 25}

3. $y = 2 + 3x$ is a linear equation. This means, for every x in the domain, there will be one and only one corresponding y in the range. As a matter of fact, for every unique x in the domain, there corresponds a unique y in the range. Therefore, $y = 2 + 3x$ is a function of x.

   Since $y = 2 + 3x$ is also a one-to-one function, it has an inverse function. To find the inverse of a one-to-one function, solve the given equation for x.

   $2 + 3x = y$

   $-2 \qquad - 2$

   $3x = y - 2$

   $\dfrac{3x}{3} = \dfrac{y-2}{3}$

   $x = \dfrac{y-2}{3} = \dfrac{y}{3} - \dfrac{2}{3}$

   $x = \dfrac{1}{3}y - \dfrac{2}{3}$

   This is a linear relationship where each y in $0 \le y < \infty$. There is one x *for each y*.

5. $z = 2w^2 + 4$ is a quadratic relationship, where each w in the domain has only one z in the range. Therefore, $z = 2w^2 + 4$ is a function of w.

Since $z = 2w^2 + 4$ is not a one-to-one function, it does not have an inverse that is a function. To verify this, solve the equation for w. We have:

$z = 2w^2 + 4$

$2w^2 + 4 = z$

$ -4 -4$

$2w^2 = z - 4$

$\dfrac{2w^2}{2} = \dfrac{z-4}{2}$

$w^2 = \dfrac{z-4}{2}$

$(w^2)^{1/2} = \pm\left(\dfrac{z-4}{2}\right)^{1/2}$

$w = \pm\sqrt{\dfrac{z-4}{2}}$

The inverse relation is not a function, because for every z in $4 \le z \le 10$, there corresponds two values of w.

7. (a) $f(2) = (2)^2 + 3(2) - 6 = 4 + 6 - 6 = 4$

(b) $f(5) = (5)^2 + 3(5) - 6 = 25 + 15 - 6 = 34$

(c) $f(0) = (0)^2 + 3(0) - 6 = 0 + 0 - 6 = -6$

(d) $f(a + b) = (a + b)^2 + 3(a + b) - 6 = (a + b)(a + b) + 3(a + b) - 6$

$ = a^2 + ab + ba + b^2 + 3a + 3b - 6$

$ = a^2 + ab + ab + b^2 + 3a + 3b - 6$

$ = a^2 + 2ab + b^2 + 3a + 3b - 6$

(e) $f(x + \Delta x) = (x + \Delta x)^2 + 3(x + \Delta x) - 6 = (x + \Delta x)(x + \Delta x) + 3(x + \Delta x) - 6$

$ = x^2 + x(\Delta x) + (\Delta x)x + 3x + 3\Delta x - 6$

$ = x^2 + x(\Delta x) + x(\Delta x) + (\Delta x)^2 + 3x + 3(\Delta x) - 6$

$ = x^2 + 3x - 6 + 2x(\Delta x) + 3(\Delta x) + (\Delta x)^2$

9. (a) $f(2) = 2 + 2(2)^2 + (2)^3 = 2 + 8 + 8 = 18$

(b) $f(d) = d + 2(d)^2 + (d)^3 = d + 2d^2 + d^3$

(c) $f(x + y) = (x + y) + 2(x + y)^2 + (x + y)^3 = x + y + 2(x + y)^2 + (x + y)^3$

(d) $f(2a) = 2a + 2(2a)^2 + (2a)^3 = 2a + 2(4a^2) + 8a^3 = 2a + 8a^2 + 8a^3$

Section 4.3: Average Rate of Change

1. For problems (a) – (d), the average rate of change in y with respect to x over $[x_1, x_2]$

$$= \frac{f(x_2) - f(x_1)}{x_2 - x_1}.$$

(a) $f(x_1) = f(1) = (1)^2 - 4(1) + 5 = 1 - 4 + 5 = 2$

$f(x_2) = f(10) = (10)^2 - 4(10) + 5 = 100 - 40 + 5 = 65$

The average rate of change $= \dfrac{f(x_2) - f(x_1)}{x_2 - x_1} = \dfrac{65 - 2}{10 - 1} = \dfrac{63}{9} = 7$

(b) $f(x_1) = f(1) = (1)^2 - 4(1) + 5 = 1 - 4 + 5 = 2$

$f(x_2) = f(8) = (8)^2 - 4(8) + 5 = 64 - 32 + 5 = 37$

The average rate of change $= \dfrac{f(x_2) - f(x_1)}{x_2 - x_1} = \dfrac{37 - 2}{8 - 1} = \dfrac{35}{7} = 5$

(c) $f(x_1) = f(-2) = (-2)^2 - 4(-2) + 5 = 4 + 8 + 5 = 17$

$f(x_2) = f(1) = (1)^2 - 4(1) + 5 = 1 - 4 + 5 = 2$

The average rate of change $= \dfrac{f(x_2) - f(x_1)}{x_2 - x_1} = \dfrac{2 - 17}{1 - (-2)} = \dfrac{-15}{1 + 2} = \dfrac{-15}{3} = -5$

(d) $f(x_1) = f(-3) = (-3)^2 - 4(-3) + 5 = 9 + 12 + 5 = 26$

$f(x_2) = f(-1) = (-1)^2 - 4(-1) + 5 = 1 + 4 + 5 = 10$

The average rate of change $= \dfrac{f(x_2) - f(x_1)}{x_2 - x_1} = \dfrac{10 - 26}{-1 - (-3)} = \dfrac{-16}{-1 + 3} = \dfrac{-16}{2} = -8$

3. (a) $f(x_1) = f(1) = 3(1) - 4 = 3 - 4 = -1$

$f(x_2) = f(5) = 3(5) - 4 = 15 - 4 = 11$

The average rate of change $= \dfrac{f(x_2) - f(x_1)}{x_2 - x_1} = \dfrac{11 - (-1)}{5 - 1} = \dfrac{11 + 1}{4} = \dfrac{12}{4} = 3$

(b) $f(x_1) = f(1) = (1)^2 + 6(1) + 2 = 1 + 6 + 2 = 9$

$f(x_2) = f(5) = (5)^2 + 6(5) + 2 = 25 + 30 + 2 = 57$

The average rate of change $= \dfrac{f(x_2) - f(x_1)}{x_2 - x_1} = \dfrac{57 - 9}{5 - 1} = \dfrac{48}{4} = 12$

(c) $y(x_1) = y(1) = (1)^3 + 5 = 1 + 5 = 6$

$y(x_2) = y(5) = (5)^3 + 5 = 125 + 5 = 130$

The average rate of change $= \dfrac{y(x_2) - y(x_1)}{x_2 - x_1} = \dfrac{130 - 6}{5 - 1} = \dfrac{124}{4} = 31$

(d) $s(t_1) = s(1) = 2 - 3(1)^2 = 2 - 3 = -1$

$s(t_2) = s(5) = 2 - 3(5)^2 - 3(25) = 2 - 75 = -73$

The average rate of change $= \dfrac{s(t_2) - s(t_1)}{t_2 - t_1} = \dfrac{-73 - (-1)}{5 - 1} = \dfrac{-73 + 1}{4} = \dfrac{-72}{4} = -18$

5. The average rate of change in y with respect to x over $[x_1, x_2]$

$$= \frac{y_2 - y_1}{x_2 - x_1} = \frac{\dfrac{1}{x_2} - \dfrac{1}{x_1}}{x_2 - x_1}$$

$$= \frac{\dfrac{1}{x_2} \cdot \dfrac{x_1}{x_1} - \dfrac{1}{x_1} \cdot \dfrac{x_2}{x_2}}{x_2 - x_1} = \frac{\dfrac{x_1}{x_1 x_2} - \dfrac{x_2}{x_1 x_2}}{x_2 - x_1} = \frac{\dfrac{x_1 - x_2}{x_1 x_2}}{x_2 - x_1} = \frac{x_1 - x_2}{x_1 x_2} \div \frac{(x_2 - x_1)}{1}$$

$$= \frac{x_1 - x_2}{x_1 x_2} \cdot \frac{1}{x_2 - x_1} = \frac{-(x_2 - x_1)}{x_1 x_2} \cdot \frac{1}{x_2 - x_1} = \frac{-1}{x_1 x_2}, \ x_1 \neq x_2$$

(a) The average rate of change on [4, 6] $= \dfrac{-1}{x_1 x_2} = \dfrac{-1}{4(6)} = -\dfrac{1}{24} = -0.04167$

(b) The average rate of change on [3, 7] $= \dfrac{-1}{x_1 x_2} = \dfrac{-1}{3(7)} = -\dfrac{1}{21} = -0.04762$

(c) The average rate of change on [2, 4] $= \dfrac{-1}{x_1 x_2} = \dfrac{-1}{2(4)} = -\dfrac{1}{8} = -0.125$

Section 4.4: Instantaneous Rates of Change

1. m = The slope of a tangent line to the curve defined by the function $f(x)$ at (x, y)

= instantaneous rate of change of $f(x)$ at $x = \lim\limits_{h \to 0} \dfrac{f(x + h) - f(x)}{h}$.

(a) First, find the slope of the tangent line to the curve defined by $f(x)$ at (x, y).

The slope of the tangent line to the curve defined by the function $f(x) = x^2 - 6x + 10$ at $(1, 5)$ = instantaneous rate of change of $f(x) = x^2 - 6x + 10$ at $x = 1$:

$$m = \lim_{h \to 0} \frac{f(1+h)-f(1)}{h}$$

$$m = \lim_{h \to 0} \frac{f(1+h)-f(1)}{h} = \lim_{h \to 0} \frac{\left[(1+h)^2 - 6(1+h)+10\right] - \left(1^2 - 6(1)+10\right)}{h}$$

$$= \lim_{h \to 0} \frac{1+2h+h^2-6-6h+10-1+6-10}{h} = \lim_{h \to 0} \frac{-4h+h^2}{h} = \lim_{h \to 0} \frac{h(-4+h)}{h} = \lim_{h \to 0}(-4+h) = -4$$

To graph the tangent line to the curve at $(1, 5)$, we will need to find its equation: $y = mx + b$. With $m = -4$, $y = -4x + b$. Use $(1, 5)$ to find b. We have:

$5 = -4(1) + b$

$5 = -4 + b$

$+4 \quad +4$

$b = 9$

The tangent line to the curve at $(1, 5)$ is $y = -4x + 9$.

x	$y = x^2 - 6x + 10$	$y = -4x + 9$
-3	37	21
-2	26	17
-1	17	13
0	10	9
0.5	7.25	7
0.55	7.0025	6.8
0.65	6.5225	6.4
0.75	6.0625	6
1	5	5
2	2	1
3	1	-3
5	5	-11
6	10	-15
7	17	-19
8	26	-23

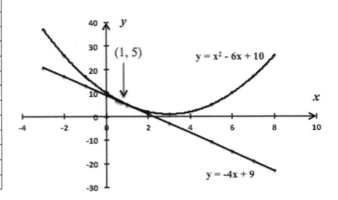

(b) First, find the slope of the tangent line to the curve defined by $f(x)$ at (x, y).

The slope of the tangent line to the curve defined by the function $f(x) = x^2 - 6x + 10$ at $(3,1)$ = instantaneous rate of change of $f(x) = x^2 - 6x + 10$ at $x = 3$:

$$m = \lim_{h \to 0} \frac{f(3+h)-f(3)}{h}.$$

$$m = \lim_{h \to 0} \frac{f(3+h)-f(3)}{h} = \lim_{h \to 0} \frac{\left[(3+h)^2 - 6(3+h)+10\right] - \left(3^2 - 6(3)+10\right)}{h}$$

$$= \lim_{h \to 0} \frac{9+6h+h^2-18-6h+10-9+18-10}{h} = \lim_{h \to 0} \frac{h^2}{h} = \lim_{h \to 0} \frac{h \cdot h}{h} = \lim_{h \to 0} h = 0.$$

To graph the tangent line to the curve at (3,1), we will need to find its equation: $y = mx + b$. With $m = 0$, $y = b$. Use (3,1) to find b. We have 1= b. The tangent line to the curve at (3,1) is $y = 1$.

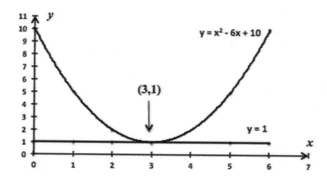

(c) First, find the slope of the tangent line to the curve defined by $f(x)$ at (x, y).

The slope of the tangent line to the curve defined by the function $f(x) = x^2 - 6x + 10$ at $(5, 5)$ = instantaneous rate of change of $f(x) = x^2 - 6x + 10$ at $x = 5$

$$m = \lim_{h \to 0} \frac{f(5+h)-f(5)}{h} = \lim_{h \to 0} \frac{\left[(5+h)^2 - 6(5+h)+10\right] - \left[5^2 - 6(5)+10\right]}{h}$$

$$= \lim_{h \to 0} \frac{25+10h+h^2-30-6h+10-25+30-10}{h} = \lim_{h \to 0} \frac{4h+h^2}{h} = \lim_{h \to 0} \frac{h(4+h)}{h} = \lim_{h \to 0}(4+h) = 4$$

To graph the tangent line to the curve at (5,5), we will need to find its equation: $y = mx + b$. With $m = 4$, use (5, 5) to find b. We have:

$$5 = 4(5) + b$$
$$5 = 20 + b$$
$$-20 \quad -20$$
$$b = -15$$

The tangent line to the curve at (5, 5) is $y = 4x - 15$.

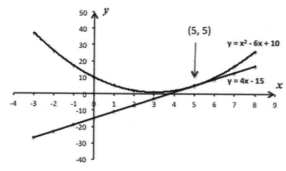

3. (a) To graph the equation, choose arbitrary x-values and then, substitute each x-value into the equation to find its corresponding y-value. Then plot the points on a graph. We have:

For $x = -4$, $y = (-4)^2 + (-4) = 16 - 4 = 12$

For $x = -3$, $y = (-3)^2 + (-3) = 9 - 3 = 6$

For $x = -2$, $y = (-2)^2 + (-2) = 4 - 2 = 2$

For $x = -1$, $y = (-1)^2 + (-1) = 1 - 1 = 0$

For $x = 0$, $\quad y = 0^2 + 0 = 0$

For $x = 1$, $\quad y = (1)^2 + 1 = 1 + 1 = 2$

For $x = 2$, $\quad y = (2)^2 + 2 = 4 + 2 = 6$

For $x = 3$, $\quad y = (3)^2 + 3 = 9 + 3 = 12$

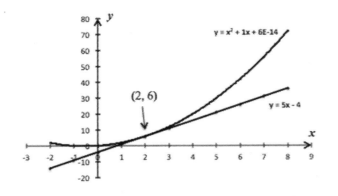

x	$y = x^2 + x$	(x, y)
-4	12	$(-4, 12)$
-3	6	$(-3, 6)$
-2	2	$(-2, 2)$
-1	0	$(-1, 0)$
0	0	$(0, 0)$
1	2	$(1, 2)$
2	6	$(2, 6)$
3	12	$(3, 12)$

(b) For $x_2 = 5.0$, $y_2 = (5.0)^2 + 5.0 = 25 + 5 = 30$

$$\frac{y_2 - y_1}{x_2 - x_1} = \frac{30 - 6}{5.0 - 2} = \frac{24}{3} = 8$$

For $x_2 = 3.0$, $y_2 = (3.0)^2 + 3.0 = 9 + 3.0 = 1$

$$\frac{y_2 - y_1}{x_2 - x_1} = \frac{12 - 6}{3.0 - 2} = \frac{6}{1} = 6$$

For $x_2 = 2.5$, $y_2 = (2.5)^2 + 2.5 = 6.25 + 2.5 = 8.75$

$$\frac{y_2 - y_1}{x_2 - x_1} = \frac{8.75 - 6}{2.5 - 2} = \frac{2.75}{.5} = 5.5$$

For $x_2 = 2.2$, $y_2 = (2.2)^2 + 2.2 = 4.84 + 2.2 = 7.04$

$$\frac{y_2 - y_1}{x_2 - x_1} = \frac{7.04 - 6}{2.2 - 2} = \frac{1.04}{.2} = 5.2$$

For $x_2 = 2.1$, $y_2 = (2.1)^2 + 2.1 = 4.41 + 2.1 = 6.5$

$$\frac{y_2 - y_1}{x_2 - x_1} = \frac{6.51 - 6}{2.1 - 2} = \frac{.51}{.1} = 5.1$$

x_1	x_2	y_1	y_2	Average rate $= \dfrac{y_2 - y_1}{x_2 - x_1}$
2	5.0	6	30	8
2	3.0	6	12	6
2	2.5	6	8.75	5.5
2	2.2	6	7.04	5.2
2	2.1	6	6.51	5.1

Yes. The slope of the tangent line to the curve $y = x^2 + x$ at $(2, 6)$ is 5.

(c) Instantaneous rate of change in $f(x)$ at any $(x, y) = m = \lim\limits_{h \to 0} \dfrac{f(x+h) - f(x)}{h}$.

$$m = \lim_{h \to 0} \frac{f(2+h) - f(2)}{h} = \lim_{h \to 0} \frac{\left[(2+h)^2 + (2+h)\right] - (2^2 + 2)}{h} = \lim_{h \to 0} \frac{4 + 4h + h^2 + 2 + h - 4 - 2}{h}$$

$$= \lim_{h \to 0} \frac{5h + h^2}{h} = \lim_{h \to 0} \frac{\cancel{h}(5+h)}{\cancel{h}} = \lim_{h \to 0}(5+h) = 5 + 0 = 5$$

5. Instantaneous rate of change in $f(x)$ at any $(x, y) = \lim\limits_{h \to 0} \dfrac{f(x+h) - f(x)}{h}$.

$$\lim_{h \to 0} \frac{f(x+h) - f(x)}{h} = \lim_{h \to 0} \frac{2 - 3(x+h) - (2 - 3x)}{h} = \lim_{h \to 0} \frac{2 - 3x - 3h - 2 + 3x}{h}$$

$$= \lim_{h \to 0} \frac{-3h}{h} = \lim_{h \to 0} \frac{-3\cancel{h}}{\cancel{h}} = \lim_{h \to 0}(-3) = -3.$$

The instantaneous rate of change at $x = 1$ is -3.

The instantaneous rate of change at $x = -5$ is -3.

7. Instantaneous rate of change in $f(x)$ at any $x = \lim\limits_{h \to 0} \dfrac{f(x+h) - f(x)}{h}$.

$$= \lim_{h \to 0} \frac{f(x+h) - f(x)}{h} = \lim_{h \to 0} \frac{\left[(x+h)^2 - 2(x+h) + 10\right] - \left(x^2 - 2x + 10\right)}{h}$$

$$= \lim_{h \to 0} \frac{x^2 + 2xh + h^2 - 2x - 2h + 10 - x^2 + 2x - 10}{h} = \lim_{h \to 0} \frac{2xh + h^2 - 2h}{h} = \lim_{h \to 0} \frac{h(2x + h - 2)}{h}$$

$$= \lim_{h \to 0} \frac{\cancel{h}(2x + h - 2)}{\cancel{h}} = \lim_{h \to 0}(2x + h - 2) = 2x + 0 - 2 = 2x - 2$$

The instantaneous rate of change at $x = 1$ is $2(1) - 2 = 0$.

The instantaneous rate of change at $x = -5$ is $2(-5) - 2 = -10 - 2 = -12$.

9. Instantaneous rate of change in $f(x)$ at any $x = \lim_{h \to 0} \dfrac{f(x+h) - f(x)}{h}$.

$$\lim_{h \to 0} \frac{f(x+h) - f(x)}{h} = \lim_{h \to 0} \frac{\left[2(x+h)^3 - 2(x+h)^2 + 3(x+h) - 1\right] - \left[2x^3 - 2x^2 + 3x - 1\right]}{h}$$

$$= \lim_{h \to 0} \frac{2\left(x^3 + 3x^2 h + 3xh^2 + h^3\right) - 2\left(x^2 + 2xh + h^2\right) + 3(x+h) - 1 - \left(2x^3 - 2x^2 + 3x - 1\right)}{h}$$

$$= \lim_{h \to 0} \frac{2x^3 + 6x^2 h + 6xh^2 + 2h^3 - 2x^2 - 4xh - 2h^2 + 3x + 3h - 1 - 2x^3 + 2x^2 - 3x + 1}{h}$$

$$= \lim_{h \to 0} \frac{6x^2 h + 6xh^2 + 2h^3 - 4xh - 2h^2 + 3h}{h} = \lim_{h \to 0} \frac{h\left(6x^2 + 6xh + 2h^2 - 4x - 2h + 3\right)}{h}, \quad h \neq 0$$

$$= \lim_{h \to 0} \left(6x^2 + 6xh + 2h^2 - 4x - 2h + 3\right) = 6x^2 + 6x(0) + 2(0)^2 - 4x - 2(0) + 3 = 6x^2 - 4x + 3$$

The instantaneous rate of change at $x = 1$ is $6(1)^2 - 4(1) + 3 = 6 - 4 + 3 = 5$.

The instantaneous rate of change at $x = -5$ is $6(-5)^2 - 4(-5) + 3 = 150 + 20 + 3 = 173$.

11. Instantaneous rate of change in $f(x)$ at any $x = \lim_{h \to 0} \dfrac{f(x+h) - f(x)}{h}$

$$= \lim_{h \to 0} \frac{f(x+h) - f(x)}{h} = \lim_{h \to 0} \frac{\dfrac{x+h}{x+h+2} - \dfrac{x}{x+2}}{h} = \lim_{h \to 0} \frac{\dfrac{x+h}{x+h+2} \cdot \dfrac{(x+2)}{(x+2)} - \dfrac{x}{x+2} \cdot \dfrac{(x+h+2)}{(x+h+2)}}{h}$$

$$= \lim_{h \to 0} \frac{\dfrac{(x+h)(x+2) - x(x+h+2)}{(x+2)(x+h+2)}}{h} = \lim_{h \to 0} \frac{\dfrac{x^2 + 2x + hx + 2h - x^2 - xh - 2x}{(x+2)(x+h+2)}}{h}$$

$$= \lim_{h \to 0} \frac{\dfrac{2h}{(x+2)(x+h+2)}}{h} = \lim_{h \to 0} \left[\frac{2h}{(x+2)(x+h+2)} \div \frac{h}{1}\right] = \lim_{h \to 0} \left[\frac{2h}{(x+2)(x+h+2)} \cdot \frac{1}{h}\right]$$

$$= \lim_{h \to 0} \frac{2}{(x+2)(x+h+2)} = \frac{2}{(x+2)(x+0+2)} = \frac{2}{(x+2)(x+2)} = \frac{2}{(x+2)^2}$$

The instantaneous rate of change at $x = 1$ is $\dfrac{2}{(1+2)^2} = \dfrac{2}{3^2} = \dfrac{2}{9}$.

The instantaneous rate of change at $x = -5$ is $\dfrac{2}{(-5+2)^2} = \dfrac{2}{(-3)^2} = \dfrac{2}{9}$.

13. Instantaneous rate of change in $f(x)$ at any $x = \lim\limits_{h \to 0} \dfrac{f(x+h) - f(x)}{h}$.

$= \lim\limits_{h \to 0} \dfrac{\dfrac{1}{(x+h)^2} - \dfrac{1}{x^2}}{h} = \lim\limits_{h \to 0} \dfrac{\dfrac{1}{(x+h)^2} \cdot \dfrac{x^2}{x^2} - \dfrac{1}{x^2} \cdot \dfrac{(x+h)^2}{(x+h)^2}}{h} = \lim\limits_{h \to 0} \dfrac{\dfrac{x^2}{x^2(x+h)^2} - \dfrac{(x+h)^2}{x^2(x+h)^2}}{h}$

$= \lim\limits_{h \to 0} \dfrac{\dfrac{x^2 - (x+h)^2}{x^2(x+h)^2}}{h} = \lim\limits_{h \to 0} \dfrac{\dfrac{x^2 - \left(x^2 + 2xh + h^2\right)}{x^2(x+h)^2}}{h} = \lim\limits_{h \to 0} \dfrac{\dfrac{x^2 - x^2 - 2xh - h^2}{x^2(x+h)^2}}{h} = \lim\limits_{h \to 0} \dfrac{\dfrac{-2xh - h^2}{x^2(x+h)^2}}{h}$

$= \lim\limits_{h \to 0} \left[\dfrac{h(-2x-h)}{x^2(x+h)^2} \div \dfrac{h}{1} \right] = \lim\limits_{h \to 0} \left[\dfrac{\cancel{h}(-2x-h)}{x^2(x+h)^2} \cdot \dfrac{1}{\cancel{h}} \right] = \lim\limits_{h \to 0} \dfrac{-2x-h}{x^2(x+h)^2} = \dfrac{-2x-0}{x^2(x+0)^2}$

$= \dfrac{-2x}{x^2 \cdot x^2} = \dfrac{-2x}{x^4} = \dfrac{-2}{x^3}$

The instantaneous rate of change at $x = 1$ is $\dfrac{-2}{(1)^3} = \dfrac{-2}{1} = -2$.

The instantaneous rate of change at $x = -5$ is $\dfrac{-2}{(-5)^3} = \dfrac{-2}{-125} = \dfrac{2}{125}$.

15. The average rate of change over $[3, 5] = \dfrac{y_2 - y_1}{x_2 - x_1} = \dfrac{7-7}{5-3} = \dfrac{0}{2} = 0$

The average rate of change over $[5, 7] = \dfrac{y_2 - y_1}{x_2 - x_1} = \dfrac{12-7}{7-5} = \dfrac{5}{2}$

The average rate of change over $[4, 5] = \dfrac{y_2 - y_1}{x_2 - x_1} = \dfrac{7-7}{5-4} = \dfrac{0}{1} = 0$

The average rate of change over $[5, 6] = \dfrac{y_2 - y_1}{x_2 - x_1} = \dfrac{12-7}{6-5} = \dfrac{5}{1} = 5$

The average rate of change over $[5, 5.3] = \dfrac{y_2 - y_1}{x_2 - x_1} = \dfrac{12-7}{5.3-5} = \dfrac{5}{0.3} = 16.7$

The average rate of change over $[5, 5.3] = \dfrac{y_2 - y_1}{x_2 - x_1} = \dfrac{12-7}{5.3-5} = \dfrac{5}{0.3} = 16.7$

The average rate of change over $[5, 5.7] = \dfrac{y_2 - y_1}{x_2 - x_1} = \dfrac{12-7}{5.7-5} = \dfrac{5}{0.7} = 7.1$

The average rate of change over $[5, 5.3] = \frac{y_2 - y_1}{x_2 - x_1} = \frac{12 - 7}{5.3 - 5} = \frac{5}{0.3} = 16.$

The average rate of change over $[5, 5.9] = \frac{y_2 - y_1}{x_2 - x_1} = \frac{12 - 7}{5.9 - 5} = \frac{5}{0.9} = 5.6$

The average rate of change over $[5, 5.1] = \frac{y_2 - y_1}{x_2 - x_1} = \frac{12 - 7}{5.1 - 5} = \frac{5}{0.1} = 50$

The average rate of change over $[5, 5.95] = \frac{y_2 - y_1}{x_2 - x_1} = \frac{12 - 7}{5.95 - 5} = \frac{5}{0.95} = 5.3$

The average rate of change over $[5, 5.05] = \frac{y_2 - y_1}{x_2 - x_1} = \frac{12 - 7}{5.05 - 5} = \frac{5}{0.05} = 100$

The average rate of change over $[5, 5.99] = \frac{y_2 - y_1}{x_2 - x_1} = \frac{12 - 7}{5.99 - 5} = \frac{5}{0.99} = 5.1$

The average rate of change over $[5, 5.01] = \frac{y_2 - y_1}{x_2 - x_1} = \frac{12 - 7}{5.01 - 5} = \frac{5}{0.01} = 500$

The instantaneous rate of change at $x = 5$ does not exist.

17. (a) Firm's average growth rate in sales on $[0, 7] = \frac{R(x_2) - R(x_1)}{x_2 - x_1}$.

$R(x_1) = R(0) = 3(0) + \frac{1}{2}(0)^2 = 0 + \frac{1}{2}(0) = 0.$

$R(x_2) = R(7) = 3(7) + \frac{1}{2}(7)^2 = 21 + \frac{1}{2}(49) = 21 + 24.5 = 45.5$

$\frac{R(x_2) - R(x_1)}{x_2 - x_1} = \frac{45.5 - 0}{7 - 0} = \$6.5$ million per year.

(b) Firm's instantaneous rate of growth $= \lim_{h \to 0} \frac{R(x + h) - R(x)}{h}$

$= \lim_{h \to 0} \left[\frac{3(x+h) + \frac{1}{2}(x+h)^2 - \left(3x + \frac{1}{2}x^2\right)}{h} \right] = \lim_{h \to 0} \frac{3x + 3h + \frac{1}{2}\left(x^2 + 2xh + h^2\right) - 3x - \frac{1}{2}x^2}{h}$

$= \lim_{h \to 0} \frac{3x + 3h + \frac{1}{2}x^2 + xh + \frac{1}{2}h^2 - 3x - \frac{1}{2}x^2}{h} = \lim_{h \to 0} \frac{3h + xh}{h} = \lim_{h \to 0} \frac{h(3 + x)}{h}$

$= \lim_{h \to 0} (3 + x) = 3 + x$

Firm's instantaneous rate of growth after its seventh year $= 3 + 7 = \$10$ million per year.

(c) $R(10) = 3(10) + \frac{1}{2}(10)^2 = 30 + \frac{1}{2}(100) = 30 + 50 = \$80$ million per year.

(d) If the growth in sales after the seventh year always equals the growth achieved at the end of the seventh year, then the firm's total sales at the end of the tenth year is $R(7) + 3(3 + 7) = \left[3(7) + \frac{1}{2}(7)^2\right] + 3(10) = 21 + \frac{1}{2}(49) + 30 = \$75.5$ million per year.

Section 4.5: The Derivative

1. $f'(x) = 5x^{5-1} - 7(3x^{3-1}) + 4 + 0 = 5x^4 - 21x^2 + 4$

3. $f'(x) = 7x^{7-1} + 6(3x^{3-1}) - 4(2x^{2-1}) = 7x^6 + 18x^2 - 8x$

5. First, rewrite $f(x)$ as $f(x) = \frac{1}{5}x^5 - \frac{1}{3}x^3 - \frac{1}{2}x^2 + 10$.

   Then, $f'(x) = \frac{1}{5}(5x^{5-1}) - \frac{1}{3}(3x^{3-1}) - \frac{1}{2}(2x^{2-1}) + 0 = \frac{5}{5}x^4 - \frac{3}{3}x^2 - \frac{2}{2}x = x^4 - x^2 - x$

7. First, expand the product by using the FOIL method.

   We have: $f(x) = x^2(x^5) + x^2(3) + 4(x^5) + 4(3) = x^7 + 3x^2 + 4x^5 + 12$

   Then, $f'(x) = 7x^{7-1} + 3(2x^{2-1}) + 4(5x^{5-1}) + 0 = 7x^6 + 6x + 20x^4 = 7x^6 + 20x^4 + 6x$

9. $f'(x) = 10 \cdot e^x = 10e^x$, since the derivative of e^x is e^x.

11. $f'(x) = 4x^{4-1} - 7(2x^{2-1}) + (7e)e^x = 4x^3 - 14x + 7e^x$

13. Using the distributive property, $f(x)$ becomes: $f(x) = x^3 + 2x^2 + 8e^x$.

    Then, $f'(x) = 3x^{3-1} + 2(2x^{2-1}) + 8e^x = 3x^2 + 4x + 8e^x$

15. First, simplify $f(x)$ by factoring the numerator. Then, cancel the factor $(x + 2)$. We have:

    $f(x) = \dfrac{(x+10)\cancel{(x+2)}}{\cancel{x+2}} = x + 10$, if $x \neq -2$. Therefore, $f'(x) = 1 + 0 = 1$.

17. $\dfrac{dy}{dx} = 7x^{7-1} + 6(5x^{5-1}) + 3 + 0 = 7x^6 + 30x^4 + 3$

19. Rewrite y to $y = x^5 - \frac{1}{4}x^4 + 7e^x$.

    Then, $\dfrac{dy}{dx} = 5x^{5-1} - \frac{1}{4}(4x^{4-1}) + 7e^x = 5x^4 - \frac{4}{4}x^3 + 7e^x = 5x^4 - x^3 + 7e^x$

21. Rewrite y to $y = \frac{1}{4}x^4 - \frac{1}{3}x^3 - \frac{1}{2}x^2$.

    Then, $\dfrac{dy}{dx} = \frac{1}{4}(4x^{4-1}) - \frac{1}{3}(3x^{3-1}) - \frac{1}{2}(2x^{2-1}) = \frac{4}{4}x^3 - \frac{3}{3}x^2 - \frac{2}{2}x = x^3 - x^2 - x$

23. Expand the product by using the FOIL method. We have:

    $y = x^2(x) - x^2(3) + 2(x) - 2(3) = x^3 - 3x^2 + 2x - 6$.

    Then, $\dfrac{dy}{dx} = 3x^{3-1} - 3(2x^{2-1}) + 2 - 0 = 3x^2 - 6x + 2$

25. (a) $S'(x) = 0 + 6,000 - 50(2x^{2-1}) = 6,000 - 100x$

(b) At $x = 45$, $S'(45) = 6,000 - 100(45) = \$6,000 - \$4,500 = \$1,500$.
Yes. At an advertising expenditure of \$45,000, there is an increase in sales at \$1,500.

At $x = 60$, $S'(60) = 6000 - 100(60) = 6000 - 6000 = \$0$. This means, if the company spends more than \$60,000 in advertising, the amount of sales will actually decline.

27. (a) Average rate of change over $[0, 4] = \dfrac{D(t_2) - D(t_1)}{t_2 - t_1} = \dfrac{2 - 0}{4 - 0} = \dfrac{2}{4}$. This means, every 2 miles traveled, it will take 4 minutes. Using dimensional analysis, we have:

$$\frac{2\ mi}{4\ min} = \frac{2\ mi}{4\ min} \cdot \frac{60\ min}{1\ hr} = \frac{120\ mi}{4\ hr} = 30 \text{ mph}$$

(b)

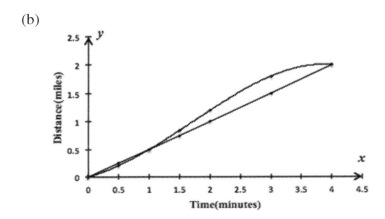

(c) $D'(t) = -0.05(3t^{3-1}) + 0.25(2t^{2-1}) + 0.3 = -0.15t^2 + 0.5t + 0.3$.

$D'(1) = -0.15(1)^2 + 0.5(1) + 0.3 = -0.15 + 0.5 + 0.3 = 0.65$

The speed of Mr. Williams' car at exactly 1 minute after the start of his trip is 0.65 mile per minute. Using dimensional analysis, we have:

$$D'(1) = \frac{0.65\ mi}{1\ min} = \frac{0.65mi}{1min} \cdot \frac{60min}{1\ hr} = \frac{39mi}{1hr} = 39 \text{ mph}.$$

(d) We need to find the equation of a tangent line to the curve
$D(t) = -0.05t^3 + 0.25t^2 + 0.3t$ at $(1, D(1)) = (1, 0.5)$. Since $m = D'(1) = 0.65$,
$y = 0.65t + b$. Use the point $(1, 0.5)$ to find b. We have:

$0.5 = 0.65(1) + b$

$0.5 = 0.65 + b$

$-0.65 \quad -0.65$

$\quad b = -0.15$

Therefore, the equation of a tangent line to the curve $D(t) = -0.05t^3 + 0.25t^2 + 0.3t$ at $(1, 0.5)$ is $y = 0.65t - 0.15$.

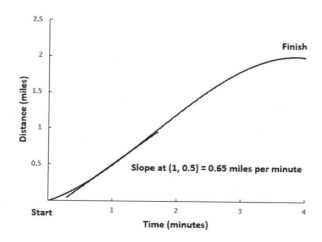

(e) $D'(4) = -0.15(4)^2 + 0.5(4) + 0.3 = -2.4 + 2 + 0.3 = -0.1$ mile per minute. Using dimensional analysis, we have:

$$D'(4) = \frac{-0.1\ mi}{1\ min} \cdot \frac{60\ min}{1\ hr} = \frac{-6\ mi}{1\ hr} = -6 \text{ miles per hour}$$

29. (a) $D'(p) = 30(2p^{2-1}) + 5 + 0 = 60p + 5 > 0, for\ p > 0$. That is, as p increases positively, $D(p)$ increases. Therefore, no.

(b) Rewrite $D(p) = 3000p^{-1}$.

Then, $D'(p) = 3000(-1p^{-1-1}) = -3000p^{-2} = \frac{-3000}{p^2}$. We see that $D'(p) < 0$ for $p > 0$. This means, when p increases positively, $D(p)$ decreases. Therefore, yes.

(c) $D'(p) = 5(2p^{2-1}) - 0 = 10p > 0$ for $p > 0$. This means, as p increases positively, $D(p)$ increases (is positive). Therefore, no.

(d) $D'(p) = 5(2p^{2-1}) - 2000 = 10p - 2000$. For $0 \le p < 200$, $D(p) < 0$(decreases). For $p > 200$, $D(p) > 0$.This means, as p increases over 200, $D(p)$ increases (is positive). Therefore, no.

Section 4.6: Additional Rules

1. There are two ways to compute $f'(x)$ for $f(x) = (x^2 + 3x)(x^5 + x^7 + 2x)$.

Method 1: Expand the product. We have:

$$f(x) = x^2(x^5 + x^7 + 2x) + 3x(x^5 + x^7 + 2x)$$

$$= x^2(x^5) + x^2(x^7) + x^2(2x) + 3x(x^5) + 3x(x^7) + 3x(2x)$$

$$= x^{2+5} + x^{2+7} + 2x^{2+1} + 3x^{1+5} + 3x^{1+7} + 6x^{1+1}$$

$$= x^7 + x^9 + 2x^3 + 3x^6 + 3x^8 + 6x^2$$

Then, $f'(x) = 7(x^{7-1}) + 9x^{9-1} + 2(3x^{3-1}) + 3(6x^{6-1}) + 3(8x^{8-1}) + 6(2x^{2-1})$

$$= 7x^6 + 9x^8 + 6x^2 + 18x^5 + 24x^7 + 12x$$

$$= 9x^8 + 24x^7 + 7x^6 + 18x^5 + 6x^2 + 12x$$

Method 2: Use the Product Rule with $g(x) = x^2 + 3x$ and $h(x) = x^5 + x^7 + 2x$.

$$f'(x) = h(x) \cdot g'(x) + g(x) \cdot h'(x)$$

$$= (x^5 + x^7 + 2x)(2x^{2-1} + 3) + (x^2 + 3x)(5x^{5-1} + 7x^{7-1} + 2)$$

$$= (x^5 + x^7 + 2x)(2x + 3) + (x^2 + 3x)(5x^4 + 7x^6 + 2)$$
$$= x^5(2x + 3) + x^7(2x + 3) + 2x(2x + 3) + x^2(5x^4 + 7x^6 + 2) + 3x(5x^4 + 7x^6 + 2)$$

$$= 2x^6 + 3x^5 + 2x^8 + 3x^7 + 4x^2 + 6x + 5x^6 + 7x^8 + 2x^2 + 15x^5 + 21x^7 + 6x$$

$$= 9x^8 + 24x^7 + 7x^6 + 18x^5 + 6x^2 + 12x$$

3. $f'(x) = -5x^{-5-1} + (-3)x^{-3-1} + (-2)x^{-2-1} = -5x^{-6} - 3x^{-4} - 2x^{-3}$

$$= -\frac{5}{x^6} - \frac{3}{x^4} - \frac{2}{x^3}$$

5. $f'(x) = -\frac{5}{2}x^{-\frac{5}{2}-1} + \left(-\frac{1}{2}\right)x^{-\frac{1}{2}-1} = -\frac{5}{2}x^{-7/2} - \frac{1}{2}x^{-3/2} = -\frac{5}{2x^{7/2}} - \frac{1}{2x^{3/2}}$

7. **(Quotient Rule)**

The derivative of the function $f(x) = \dfrac{N(x)}{D(x)}$ is $f'(x) = \dfrac{D(x) \cdot N'(x) - N(x) \cdot D'(x)}{[D(x)]^2}$,

with $N(x) = x^3 + x^5$ and $D(x) = x^2 + x^4$. We have:

$$f'(x) = \frac{(x^2 + x^4)(3x^{3-1} + 5x^{5-1}) - (x^3 + x^5)(2x^{2-1} + 4x^{4-1})}{(x^2 + x^4)^2}$$

$$= \frac{(x^2 + x^4)(3x^2 + 5x^4) - (x^3 + x^5)(2x + 4x^3)}{(x^2 + x^4)^2}$$

$$= \frac{x^2(3x^2 + 5x^4) + x^4(3x^2 + 5x^4) - x^3(2x + 4x^3) - x^5(2x + 4x^3)}{(x^2 + x^4)^2}$$

$$= \frac{x^2(3x^2)+x^2(5x^4)+x^4(3x^2)+x^4(5x^4)-x^3(2x)-x^3(4x^3)-x^5(2x)-x^5(4x^3)}{(x^2+x^4)^2}$$

$$= \frac{3x^4+5x^6+3x^6+5x^8-2x^4-4x^6-2x^6-4x^8}{(x^2+x^4)^2}$$

$$= \frac{x^8+2x^6+x^4}{(x^2+x^4)^2}$$

9. **(Quotient Rule)**

The derivative of the function $f(x) = \frac{N(x)}{D(x)}$ is $f'(x) = \frac{D(x) \cdot N'(x) - N(x) \cdot D'(x)}{[D(x)]^2}$,

with $N(x) = e^{4x}$ and $D(x) = x^5 - x^{-3}$. We have:

$$f'(x) = \frac{(x^5-x^{-3})(4e^{4x})-(e^{4x})(5x^{5-1}-(-3)x^{-3-1})}{(x^5-x^{-3})^2}$$

$$= \frac{(x^5-x^{-3})(4e^{4x})-(e^{4x})(5x^4+3x^{-4})}{(x^5-x^{-3})^2}$$

$$= \frac{x^5(4e^{4x})-x^{-3}(4e^{4x})-e^{4x}(5x^4)-e^{4x}(3x^{-4})}{(x^5-x^{-3})^2}$$

$$= \frac{4x^5e^{4x}-4x^{-3}e^{4x}-5x^4e^{4x}-3x^{-4}e^{4x}}{(x^5-x^{-3})^2}$$

11. **(Product Rule)**

The derivative of $f(x) = g(x) \cdot h(x)$ is $f'(x) = h(x) \cdot g'(x) + g(x) \cdot h'(x)$, with $g(x) = e^{7x}$ and $h(x) = x^7$. We have:

$$f'(x) = x^7(7e^{7x}) + e^{7x}(7x^{7-1}) = 7x^7e^{7x} + 7x^6e^{7x} = 7x^6e^{7x}(x+1)$$

13. The derivative of the function $f(x) = \frac{N(x)}{D(x)}$ is $f'(x) = \frac{D(x) \cdot N'(x) - N(x) \cdot D'(x)}{[D(x)]^2}$,

with $g(x) = x^6 + 7$ and $h(x) = x^5 + 3x$. We have:

$$f'(x) = \frac{(x^5+3x)(6x^{6-1}+0)-(x^6+7)(5x^{5-1}+3)}{(x^5+3x)^2}$$

$$= \frac{(x^5+3x)(6x^5)-(x^6+7)(5x^4+3)}{(x^5+3x)^2}$$

$$= \frac{x^5(6x^5)+3x(6x^5)-x^6(5x^4+3)-7(5x^4+3)}{(x^5+3x)^2}$$

$$= \frac{6x^{10}+18x^6-x^6(5x^4)-x^6(3)-7(5x^4)-7(3)}{(x^5+3x)^2}$$

$$= \frac{6x^{10}+18x^6-5x^{10}-3x^6-35x^4-21}{(x^5+3x)^2} = \frac{x^{10}+15x^6-35x^4-21}{(x^5+3x)^2}$$

$$= \frac{x^{10}+15x^6-35x^4-21}{x^{10}+6x^6+9x^2}$$

15. $f'(x) = 5(x^7+6x)^{5-1} \cdot \frac{d}{dx}(x^7+6x)$

$\qquad = 5(x^7+6x)^4(7x^{7-1}+6) = 5(x^7+6x)^4(7x^6+6)$

17. $f'(x) = 3(x^4+3x^2+4x+2)^{3-1}\frac{d}{dx}(x^4+3x^2+4x+2)$

$\qquad = 3(x^4+3x^2+4x+2)^2(4x^{4-1}+3(2x^{2-1})+4+0)$

$\qquad = 3(x^4+3x^2+4x+2)^2(4x^3+6x+4)$

19. (**Product Rule**)

The derivative of $y = g(x) \cdot h(x)$ is $\frac{dy}{dx} = h(x) \cdot g'(x) + g(x) \cdot h'(x)$, with
$g(x) = e^{10x}$ and $h(x) = x^3$.

$\frac{dy}{dx} = x^3(10e^{10x}) + e^{10x}(3x^{3-1}) = 10x^3e^{10x} + 3x^2e^{10x} = x^2e^{10x}(10x+3)$

21. $\frac{dy}{dx} = 5x^{5-1} + 3(-5x^{-5-1}) = 5x^4 - 15x^{-6} = 5x^4 - \frac{15}{x^6}$

23. First, rewrite y as $y = x^{-5} + x^{-4}$. Then,

$\frac{dy}{dx} = -5x^{-5-1} + (-4x^{-4-1}) = -5x^{-6} - 4x^{-5} = \frac{-5}{x^6} - \frac{4}{x^5}$

25. $\frac{dy}{dx} = \frac{3}{2}x^{\frac{3}{2}-1} + 7\left(\frac{5}{2}x^{\frac{5}{2}-1}\right) = \frac{3}{2}x^{1/2} + \left(7 \cdot \frac{5}{2}\right)x^{3/2} = \frac{3}{2}x^{1/2} + \frac{35}{2}x^{3/2}$

27. $\frac{dS}{dx} = \frac{dS}{dE} \cdot \frac{dE}{dx} = (2E^{2-1}+3)(2x^{2-1}) = (2E+3)(2x) = (2x^2+3)(2x)$

$\qquad = 4x^3 + 6x$

29. $\frac{dS}{dx} = \frac{dS}{dE} \cdot \frac{dE}{dx} = \left[\frac{(E+2)(1)-E(1)}{(E+2)^2}\right] \cdot (3 \cdot 2x^{2-1}) = \left[\frac{E+2-E}{(E+2)^2}\right] \cdot (3 \cdot 2x^{2-1}) = \left[\frac{2}{(E+2)^2}\right] \cdot 6x$

$= \frac{2}{(E+2)^2} \cdot \frac{6x}{1} = \frac{12x}{(E+2)^2} = \frac{12x}{(3x^2+5+2)^2} = \frac{12x}{(3x^2+7)^2} = \frac{12x}{9x^4+42x^2+49}$

Section 4.7: Higher Order Derivatives

1. **Part 1**

$\frac{dy}{dx} = 5x^{5-1} + 4(2x^{2-1}) + 3 = 5x^4 + 8x + 3$

$\frac{d^2y}{dx^2} = \frac{d}{dx}(5x^4 + 8x + 3) = 5(4x^{4-1}) + 8 + 0 = 20x^3 + 8$

Part 2

For $x = 1, \frac{d^2y}{dx^2} = 20(1)^3 + 8 = 20 + 8 = 28.$

For $x = 2, \frac{d^2y}{dx^2} = 20(2)^3 + 8 = 20 \cdot 8 + 8 = 160 + 8 = 168.$

3. **Part 1**

$\frac{dy}{dx} = 4x^{4-1} + 3(2x^{2-1}) + 4 + 0 = 4x^3 + 6x + 4$

$\frac{d^2y}{dx^2} = \frac{d}{dx}(4x^3 + 6x + 4) = 4(3x^{3-1}) + 6 + 0 = 12x^2 + 6$

Part 2

For $x = 1, \frac{d^2y}{dx^2} = 12(1)^2 + 6 = 12 + 6 = 18$

For $x = 2, \frac{d^2y}{dx^2} = 12(2)^2 + 6 = 12(4) + 6 = 48 + 6 = 54$

5. **Part 1** (**Product Rule**)

The derivative of $y = g(x) \cdot h(x)$ is $\frac{dy}{dx} = h(x) \cdot g'(x) + g(x) \cdot h'(x)$, with $g(x) = x^3$ and $h(x) = e^{10x}$.

$\frac{dy}{dx} = e^{10x}(3x^{3-1}) + x^3(10e^{10x}) = 3x^2e^{10x} + 10x^3e^{10x} = (3x^2 + 10x^3)e^{10x}$

Apply the Product Rule again for each term in $\dfrac{dy}{dx}$.

$$\frac{d^2y}{dx^2} = \frac{d}{dx}(3x^2 + 10x^3)e^{10x}$$

$$= (3x^2 + 10x^3)(10e^{10x}) + e^{10x}(3 \cdot 2x^{2-1} + 10 \cdot 3x^{3-1})$$

$$= 10(3x^2 + 10x^3)e^{10x} + e^{10x}(6x + 30x^2)$$

$$= 30x^2e^{10x} + 100x^3e^{10x} + 6xe^{10x} + 30x^2e^{10x} = 6xe^{10x} + 60x^2e^{10x} + 100x^3e^{10x}$$

$$= (6x + 60x^2 + 100x^3)e^{10x}$$

Part 2

For $x = 1$, $\dfrac{d^2y}{dx^2} = [6(1) + 60(1)^2 + 100(1)^3]e^{10(1)} = (6 + 60 + 100)e^{10} = 166e^{10}$

For $x = 2$, $\dfrac{d^2y}{dx^2} = [6(2) + 60(2)^2 + 100(2)^3]e^{10(1)} = (12 + 240 + 800)e^{20} = 1052e^{20}$

7. (a) $speed = D'(t) = -0.05(3t^{3-1}) + 0.25(2t^{2-1}) + 0.3 = -0.15t^2 + 0.5t + 0.3$

   (b) $D'(1) = -0.15(1)^2 + 0.5(1) + 0.3 = -0.15 + 0.5 + 0.3 = 0.65$. The speed of Mr. Williams' car at exactly 1 minute after the start of his trip is 0.65 mile per minute. Using dimensional analysis, we have:

   $$D'(1) = \frac{0.65\ mi}{1\ min} = \frac{0.65 mi}{1 min} \cdot \frac{60 min}{1\ hr} = \frac{39 mi}{1 hr} = 39 \text{ mph.}$$

   (c) Acceleration $= D''(t) = \dfrac{d^2D}{dt^2} = \dfrac{d}{dx}\left(-0.15t^2 + 0.5t + 0.3\right) = -0.15(2t^{2-1}) + 0.5$

   $$= -0.3t + 0.5$$

   (d) At $t = 1$, $D''(1) = -0.3(1) + 0.5 = -0.3 + 0.5 = 0.2$ mile per minute^2. Using dimensional analysis, we have:

   $$D''(1) = \frac{0.2\ mi}{1\ min} = \frac{0.2\ mi}{1 min^2} \cdot \frac{60 min}{1\ hr} \cdot \frac{60 min}{1\ hr} = \frac{mi}{hr^2} = 720 \text{ mph}^2.$$

   At $t = 3$, $D''(3) = -0.3(3) + 0.5 = -0.9 + 0.5 = -0.4$ mile per minute^2. Using dimensional analysis, we have:

   $$D''(3) = \frac{-0.4\ mi}{1\ min} = \frac{-0.4\ mi}{1 min} \cdot \frac{60 min}{1\ hr} \cdot \frac{60 min}{1\ hr} = \frac{-1440\ mi}{hr^2} = -1440 \text{ mph}^2. \text{ This means,}$$

   Mr. William had decreased his speed(decelerated) by 1440 mph^2 in 3 minutes.

Chapter 5 Applications of the Derivative

Section 5.1: Optimization through Differentiation

1.

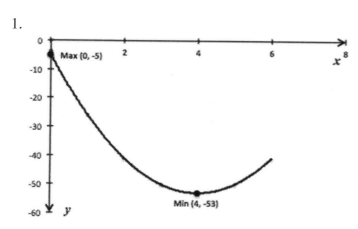

Differentiating the given function, we have: $\dfrac{dy}{dx} = 3(2x^{2-1}) - 24 - 0 = 6x - 24$. To locate all values of x for which the derivative is 0, we set the derivative function to zero and solve for x.

$6x - 24 = 0$

$\quad +24 \ + 24$

$6x = 24$

$\dfrac{6x}{6} = \dfrac{24}{6}$

$x = 4$

The derivative exists everywhere, and the endpoints are $x = 0$ and $x = 6$. Evaluating the function at $x = 0$, $x = 4$, and $x = 6$, we have:

$x = 0$, $y = 3(0)^2 - 24(0) - 5 = 0 - 0 - 5 = -5$

$x = 4$, $y = 3(4)^2 - 24(4) - 5 = 48 - 96 - 5 = -53$

$x = 6$, $y = 3(6)^2 - 24(6) - 5 = 108 - 144 - 5 = -41$

It follows that the maximum is $y = -5$ occurring at $x = 0$, and the minimum is $y = -53$ occurring at $x = 4$.

3.

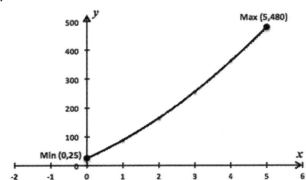

Differentiating the given function, we have: $\frac{dy}{dx} = 7(2x^{2-1}) + 56 + 0 = 14x + 56$. To locate all values of x for which the derivative is 0, we set the derivative to zero and solve for x.

$$14x + 56 = 0$$
$$\quad\;\; -56 \quad -56$$
$$14x = -56$$
$$\frac{14x}{14} = \frac{-56}{14}$$
$$x = -4$$

Because $x = -4$ is outside our domain and is not an allowable point for this problem, we disregard it. The derivative exists everywhere, and the endpoints are $x = 0$ and $x = 5$. Evaluating the function at $x = 0$ and $x = 5$, we have:

$x = 0, y = 7(0)^2 + 56(0) + 25 = 25$

$x = 5, y = 7(5)^2 + 56(5) + 25 = 175 + 280 + 25 = 480$

It follows that the maximum is $y = 480$ occurring at $x = 5$, and the minimum is $y = 25$ occurring at $x = 0$.

5.

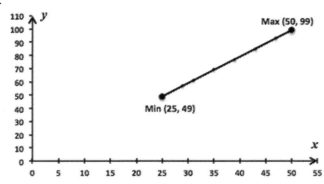

Differentiating the given function, we have $\dfrac{dy}{dx} = 2 > 0$. The derivative is 2 everywhere and never equals 0. Therefore, maximum and minimum will occur at the endpoints $x = 25$ and $x = 50$. Evaluating the function at $x = 25$ and $x = 50$, we have:

$x = 25, y = 2(25) - 1 = 50 - 1 = 49$

$x = 50, y = 2(50) - 1 = 100 - 1 = 99$

It follows that the maximum is $y = 99$ occurring at $x = 50$, and the minimum is $y = 49$ occurring at $x = 25$.

7. Differentiating the given function, we have: $D'(t) = 3t^{3-1} - 12 + 0 = 3t^2 - 12$. To locate all values of t for which the derivative is 0, we set the derivative to zero and solve for t.

$3t^2 - 12 = 0$

$3(t^2 - 4) = 0$

$3(t + 2)(t - 2) = 0$

$t + 2 = 0$ or $t - 2 = 0$

$t = -2$ or $t = 2$

$t = -2$ and $t = 2$ are both in the interval $-4 \leq t \leq 4$. Therefore, the values will be included in calculating possible maximum and minimum values. The derivative exists everywhere, and the endpoints are $t = -4$ and $t = 4$. Evaluating the function at $t = -4$, $t = -2, t = 2$, and $t = 4$, we have:

$t = -4, D = (-4)^3 - 12(-4) + 7 = -64 + 48 + 7 = -9$

$t = -2, D = (-2)^3 - 12(-2) + 7 = -8 + 24 + 7 = 23$

$t = 2, D = (2)^3 - 12(2) + 7 = 8 - 24 + 7 = -9$

$t = 4, D = (4)^3 - 12(4) + 7 = 64 - 48 + 7 = 23$

It follows that the maximum is $D = 23$ occurring at $t = -2$ and $t = 4$, and the minimum is $D = -9$ occurring at $t = -4$ and $t = 2$.

9. Differentiating the given function, we have $D'(t) = 3t^{3-1} - 12 + 0 = 3t^2 - 12$. To locate all values of t for which the derivative is 0, we set the derivative to zero and solve for t.

$3t^2 - 12 = 0$

$3(t^2 - 4) = 0$

$3(t + 2)(t - 2) = 0$

$t + 2 = 0$ or $t - 2 = 0$

$t = -2$ or $t = 2$

Because $t = -2$ is outside our domain and is not an allowable point for this problem, we disregard it. The derivative exists everywhere, and the endpoints are $t = 0$ and $t = 3$. Evaluating the function at $t = 0, t = 2$, and $t = 3$, we have:

$t = 0, D = (0)^3 - 12(0) + 7 = 0 - 0 + 7 = 7$

$t = 2, D = (2)^3 - 12(2) + 7 = 8 - 24 + 7 = -9$

$t = 3, D = (3)^3 - 12(3) + 7 = 27 - 36 + 7 = -2$

It follows that the maximum is $D = 7$ occurring at $t = 0$, and the minimum is $D = -9$ occurring at $t = 2$.

11. Differentiating the given function, we have:

$$y'(t) = 3t^{3-1} + 3(2t^{2-1}) - 105 + 0 = 3t^2 + 6t - 105$$

To locate all values of t for which the derivative is 0, we set the derivative to zero and solve for t.

$3t^2 + 6t - 105 = 0$ $t + 7 = 0$ *or* $t - 5 = 0$

$3(t^2 + 2t - 35) = 0$ $t = -7$ $t = 5$

$3(t + 7)(t - 5) = 0$

$t = -7$ *and* $t = 5$ are both in the interval $-10 \le t \le 10$. Therefore, the values will be included in calculating possible maximum and minimum values.

The derivative exists everywhere, and the endpoints are $t = -10$ and $t = 10$. Evaluating the function at $t = -10, t = -7, t = 5$, and $t = 10$, we have:

$t = -10, \ y(-10) = (-10)^3 + 3(-10)^2 - 105(-10) + 20 = 370$

$t = -7, \ y(-7) = (-7)^3 + 3(-7)^2 - 105(-7) + 20 = 559$

$t = 5, \ y(5) = (5)^3 + 3(5)^2 - 105(5) + 20 = -305$

$t = 10, \ y(10) = (10)^3 + 3(10)^2 - 105(10) + 20 = 270$

It follows that the maximum is $y = 559$ occurring at $t = -7$, and the minimum is $y = -305$ occurring at $t = 5$.

13. Differentiating the given function, we have:

$x'(t) = \frac{1}{3}(3t^{3-1}) - 4(2t^{2-1}) + 0 = \frac{3}{3}t^2 - 8t = t^2 - 8t$. To locate all values of t for which the derivative is 0, we set the derivative to zero and solve for t.

$$t^2 - 8t = 0$$

$$t(t - 8) = 0$$

$$t = 0 \ \text{ or } \ t - 8 = 0$$

$$t = 0 \ \text{ or } \ t = 8$$

The derivative exists everywhere, and the endpoints are $t = 0$ and $t = 9$. Evaluating the function at $t = 0$, $t = 8$, and $t = 9$, we have:

$$t = 0, x = \frac{1}{3}(0)^3 - 4(0)^2 + 12 = 0 - 0 + 12 = 12$$

$$t = 8, x = \frac{1}{3}(8)^3 - 4(8)^2 + 12 = \frac{512}{3} - 256 + 12 = \frac{512}{3} - 244 = \frac{512}{3} - \frac{732}{3} = -\frac{220}{3}$$

$$t = 9, x = \frac{1}{3}(9)^3 - 4(9)^2 + 12 = \frac{729}{3} - 324 + 12 = \frac{729}{3} - 312 = \frac{729}{3} - \frac{936}{3} = -\frac{207}{3} = -67$$

It follows that the maximum is $x = 12$ occurring at $t = 0$, and the minimum is $x = -\frac{220}{3}$ occurring at $t = 8$.

15. This problem can be solved by two methods.

Method 1: Expanding the Product

Expanding the product, we have $y(x) = x^2 - 20x - 10x + 200 = x^2 - 30x + 200$. Differentiating the given function, we have $y'(x) = 2x^{2-1} - 30 + 0 = 2x - 30$. To locate all values of x for which the derivative is 0, we set the derivative to zero and solve for x.

$$2x - 30 = 0$$

$$2x = 30$$

$$\frac{2x}{2} = \frac{30}{2}$$

$$x = 15$$

Method 2: Using the Product Rule

The derivative of $y = g(x) \cdot h(x)$ with $g(x) = x - 10$ and $h(x) = x - 20$ is:

$$f'(x) = h(x) \cdot g'(x) + g(x) \cdot h'(x)$$
$$= (x - 20)(1) + (x - 10)(1) = x - 20 + x - 10 = 2x - 30.$$

To locate all values of x for which the derivative is 0, we set the derivative to zero and solve for x. We have:

$$2x - 30 = 0 \qquad\qquad\qquad \frac{2x}{2} = \frac{30}{2}$$
$$\underline{+30 \quad +30} \qquad\qquad\qquad\quad x = 15$$
$$2x = 30$$

The derivative exists everywhere, and the endpoints are $x = 5$ and $x = 25$. Evaluating the function at $x = 5$, $x = 15$, and $x = 25$, we have:

$x = 5$, $y = (5 - 10)(5 - 20) = (-5)(-15) = 75$

$x = 15$, $y = (15 - 10)(15 - 20) = (5)(-5) = -25$

$x = 25$, $y = (25 - 10)(25 - 20) = (15)(5) = 75$

It follows that the maximum is $y = 75$ occurring at $x = 5$ and $x = 25$, and the minimum is $y = -25$ occurring at $x = 15$.

17. (a) Rewrite the given function as $P = 22x - \frac{1}{2,000}x^2 - 10,000$. Differentiating the given function, we have:

$$P'(x) = 22 - \frac{1}{2,000}(2x^{2-1}) - 0 = 22 - \frac{2}{2,000}x = 22 - \frac{1}{1,000}x.$$

To locate all values of x for which the derivative is 0, we set the derivative to zero and solve for x.

$22 - \frac{1}{1,000}x = 0$

$22 = \frac{1}{1,000}x$

$22 \cdot 1,000 = 1,000 \cdot \frac{1}{1,000}x$

$22,000 = \frac{\cancel{1,000}x}{\cancel{1,000}}$

$x = 22,000$ items

(b) If the manufacturer produced 22,000 items, its maximum profit is

$$P(22,000) = 22(22,000) - \frac{(22,000)^2}{2,000} - 10,000 = 484,000 - 242,000 - 10,000$$
$$= \$232,000$$

19. (a) Profit = Revenue – Total Cost

$$P(x) = 300x - (2.5x^2 - 200x + 20,000) = 300x - 2.5x^2 + 200x - 20,000$$
$$= -2.5x^2 + 500x - 20,000.$$

Differentiating the given function, we have:

$P'(x) = -2.5(2x^{2-1}) + 500 - 0 = -5x + 500.$

To locate all values of x for which the derivative is 0, we set the derivative to zero and solve for x.

$-5x + 500 = 0$

$-5x = -500$

$\frac{-5x}{-5} = \frac{-500}{-5}$

$x = 100$ refrigerators

(b) If the manufacturer produces 100 refrigerators, the profit is:

$$P(100) = -2.5(100)^2 + 500(100) - 20,000$$

$$= -25,000 + 50,000 - 20,000 = \$5,000$$

(c) $C(100) = 2.5(100)^2 - 200(100) + 20,000 = 25,000 - 20,000 + 20,000 = \$25,000$

21. Profit = Revenue – Total Cost

$$P(x) = 325x - \left(\frac{1}{3}x^3 - 10x^2 - 800x + 12,000\right)$$

$$= 325x - \frac{1}{3}x^3 + 10x^2 + 800x - 12,000$$

$$= -\frac{1}{3}x^3 + 10x^2 + 1,125x - 12,000.$$

Differentiating the given function, we have:

$$P'(x) = -\frac{1}{3}(3x^{3-1}) + 10(2x^{2-1}) + 1,125 - 0 = -\frac{3}{3}x^2 + 20x + 1,125$$

$$= -x^2 + 20x + 1,125$$

To locate all values of x for which the derivative is 0, we set the derivative to zero and solve for x.

$$-x^2 + 20x + 1,125 = 0$$

Use the quadratic formula, with $a = -1, b = 20$, and $c = 1,125$, to solve for x.

$$x = \frac{-b \pm \sqrt{b^2 - 4ac}}{2a} = \frac{-20 \pm \sqrt{(20)^2 - 4(-1)(1,125)}}{2(-1)} = \frac{-20 \pm \sqrt{400 + 4,500}}{-2}$$

$$= \frac{-20 \pm \sqrt{4,900}}{-2} = \frac{-20 \pm 70}{-2}$$

$$x = \frac{-20 + 70}{-2} = \frac{50}{-2} = -25 \quad \text{or} \quad x = \frac{-20 - 70}{-2} = \frac{-90}{-2} = 45$$

Since x represents the number of units produced/sold, it cannot be negative. Therefore, the only solution is 45 units.

23. For $0 \leq x \leq 2$, differentiate the function $y(x) = -x^2 + 2x + 5$. We have $y'(x) = -2x^{2-1} + 2 + 0 = -2x + 2$. To locate all values of x for which the derivative is 0, we set the derivative to zero and solve for x.

$$-2x + 2 = 0$$

$$-2x = -2$$

$$\frac{-2x}{-2} = \frac{-2}{-2}$$

$$x = 1$$

For $2 < x \leq 5$, differentiate the function $y(x) = x^2 - 8x + 16$. We have $y'(x) = 2x^{2-1} - 8 + 0 = 2x - 8$. To locate all values of x for which the derivative is 0, we set the derivative to zero and solve for x.

$$2x - 8 = 0$$

$$2x = 8$$

$$\frac{2x}{2} = \frac{8}{2}$$

$$x = 4$$

Evaluating the function at $x = 0$, $x = 1$, $x = 2$, $x = 4$, and $x = 5$ we have:

$$x = 0, y = -(0)^2 + 2(0) + 5 = 0 + 0 + 5 = 5$$

$$x = 1, y = -(1)^2 + 2(1) + 5 = -1 + 2 + 5 = 6$$

$$x = 2, y = -(2)^2 + 2(2) + 5 = -4 + 4 + 5 = 5$$

$$x = 4, y = (4)^2 - 8(4) + 16 = 16 - 32 + 16 = 0$$

$$x = 5, y = (5)^2 - 8(5) + 16 = 25 - 40 + 16 = 1$$

It follows that the maximum is $y = 6$ occurring at $x = 1$, and the minimum is $y = 0$ occurring at $x = 4$. (See Figure 1)

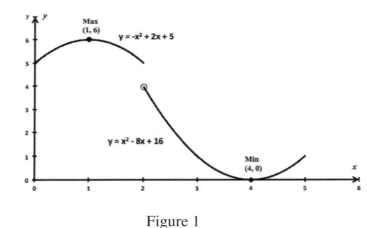

Figure 1

25. From Figure 5.4, relative minima are 5 at t = 0, 3 at $t = 2$, 2 at $t = 6$, and 3.5 at $t = 9$

27. No; No

29. First, find the derivative of the function $y(x) = x^3 - 21x^2 + 120x - 100$. We have:

$$y'(x) = 3x^{3-1} - 21(2x^{2-1}) + 120 - 0 = 3x^2 - 42x + 120.$$

To locate all values of x for which the derivative is 0, we set the derivative to zero and solve for x. We have:

$$3x^2 - 42x + 120 = 0$$
$$3(x^2 - 14x + 40) = 0$$
$$\frac{3(x^2 - 14x + 40)}{3} = \frac{0}{3}$$
$$x^2 - 14x + 40 = 0$$
$$(x - 10)(x - 4) = 0$$

$$x - 10 = 0 \qquad or \qquad x - 4 = 0$$
$$\underline{+10 \ \ +10} \qquad\qquad \underline{+4 \ \ +4}$$
$$x = 10 \qquad\qquad\qquad x = 4$$

Next, find the second derivative of the function $y(x) = x^3 - 21x^2 + 120x - 100$. We have:

$$y''(x) = \frac{d}{dx}(3x^2 - 42x + 120) = 3(2x^{2-1}) - 42 + 0 = 6x - 42.$$

For $x = 4, y''(4) = 6(4) - 42 = 24 - 42 = -18 < 0$. Therefore, a relative maximum occurs at $x = 4$. To find the relative maximum, substitute $x = 4$ into the function $y(x) = x^3 - 21x^2 + 120x - 100$. We have:

relative maximum: $y(4) = (4)^3 - 21(4)^2 + 120(4) - 100 = 108$

For $x = 10, y''(10) = 6(10) - 42 = 60 - 42 = 18 > 0$. Therefore, a relative minimum occurs at $x = 10$. To find the relative minimum, substitute $x = 10$ into the function $y(x) = x^3 - 21x^2 + 120x - 100$. We have:

relative minimum: $y(10) = (10)^3 - 21(10)^2 + 120(10) - 100 = 0$

Section 5.3: Maximizing Sales Profit

1. (a) Profit = Revenue − Total Cost

$$P(x) = 200x - \left(5,000 + 20x + \frac{1}{2}x^2\right)$$
$$= 200x - 5,000 - 20x - \frac{1}{2}x^2$$
$$= -\frac{1}{2}x^2 + 180x - 5,000$$

(b) Domain: $0 \le x \le 300$

(c) Differentiating the given function, we have:

$$P'(x) = -\frac{1}{2}(2x^{2-1}) + 180 - 0 = -\frac{2}{2}x + 180 = -x + 180.$$

To locate all values of x for which the derivative is 0, we set the derivative to zero and solve for x. We have:

$$-x + 180 = 0$$

$$\underline{-180 \quad -180}$$

$$-x = -180$$

$$x = 180$$

The derivative exists everywhere, and the endpoints are $x = 0$ and $x = 300$. Evaluating the function at $x = 0$, $x = 180$, and $x = 300$, we have:

$$x = 0, P(0) = -\frac{1}{2}(0)^2 + 180(0) - 5{,}000 = -\$5{,}000$$

$$x = 180, P(180) = -\frac{1}{2}(180)^2 + 180(180) - 5{,}000 = \$11{,}200$$

$$x = 300, P(300) = -\frac{1}{2}(300)^2 + 180(300) - 5{,}000 = \$4{,}000$$

If the manufacturer sells 180 units per week, its profit is $11,200.

3. (a) Profit = Revenue – Total Cost

$$P(x) = 10x - \left(\frac{1}{4{,}000}x^2 - 5x + 50{,}000\right) = 10x - \frac{1}{4{,}000}x^2 + 5x - 50{,}000$$

$$= -\frac{1}{4{,}000}x^2 + 15x - 50{,}000$$

(b) Domain: $0 \le x \le 50{,}000$.

(c) Differentiating the given function, we have:

$$P'(x) = -\frac{1}{4{,}000}(2x^{2-1}) + 15 - 0 = -\frac{2}{4{,}000}x + 15 = -\frac{1}{2{,}000}x + 15.$$

To locate all values of x for which the derivative is 0, we set the derivative to zero and solve for x.

$$-\frac{1}{2{,}000}x + 15 = 0 \qquad\qquad \frac{1}{2{,}000}x = 15$$

$$\underline{\quad -15 \quad -15} \qquad\qquad 2{,}000 \cdot \frac{1}{2{,}000}x = 15(2{,}000)$$

$$-\frac{1}{2{,}000}x = -15 \qquad\qquad \frac{\cancel{2000}}{\cancel{2{,}000}}x = 30{,}000$$

$$\left(-\frac{1}{2{,}000}x\right) = -(-15) \qquad\qquad x = 30{,}000 \text{ units}$$

The derivative exists everywhere, and the endpoints are $x = 0$ and $x = 50{,}000$. Evaluating the function at $x = 0$, $x = 30{,}000$, and $x = 50{,}000$, we have:

$$x = 0, P(0) = -\frac{1}{4{,}000}(0)^2 + 15(0) - 50{,}000 = 0 + 0 - 50{,}000 = -\$50{,}000$$

$$x = 30{,}0000, P(30{,}000) = -\frac{1}{4{,}000}(30{,}000)^2 + 15(30{,}000) - 50{,}000 = \$175{,}000$$

$x = 50{,}000, P(50{,}000) = -\frac{1}{4{,}000}(50{,}000)^2 + 15(50{,}000) - 50{,}000 = \$75{,}000$

If the company sells 30,000 units, its profit is $175,000.

5. Differentiating the cost function, we have:

$C'(x) = \frac{1}{4{,}000}(2x^{2-1}) - 5 + 0 = \frac{2}{4{,}000}x - 5 = \frac{1}{2{,}000}x - 5.$

To locate all values of x for which the derivative is 0, we set the derivative to zero and solve for x.

$\frac{1}{2{,}000}x - 5 = 0$

$2{,}000 \cdot \frac{1}{2{,}000}x = 5(2{,}000)$

$\frac{1}{2{,}000}x = 5$

$\frac{2000}{2{,}000}x = 10{,}000$

$x = 10{,}000$ units

The derivative exists everywhere, and the endpoints are $x = 0$ and $x = 50{,}000$. Evaluating the function at $x = 0, x = 10{,}000$, and $x = 50{,}000$, we have:

$x = 0, C(0) = \frac{(0)^2}{4{,}000} - 5(0) + 50{,}000 = 0 - 5 + 50{,}000 = \$50{,}000$

$x = 10{,}000, C(10{,}000) = \frac{(10{,}000)^2}{4{,}000} - 5(10{,}000) + 50{,}000$

$= 25{,}000 - 50{,}000 + 50{,}000 = \$25{,}000$

$x = 50{,}000, C(50{,}000) = \frac{(50{,}000)^2}{4{,}000} - 5(50{,}000) + 50{,}000$

$= 625{,}000 - 250{,}000 + 50{,}000 = \$425{,}000$

To minimize costs, the company should sell 10,000 units.

7. (a) $R(x) = (100 - 2x)x = 100x - 2x^2$

(b) Profit = Revenue – Cost

$P(x) = 100x - 2x^2 - (300x + 900) = 100x - 2x^2 - 300x - 900$
$= -2x^2 - 200x - 900$

(c) Domain: $0 \le x \le 40$

(d) Differentiating the profit function, we have:

$P'(x) = -2(2x^{2-1}) - 200 - 0 = -4x - 200$

To locate all values of x for which the derivative is 0, we set the derivative to zero and solve for x.

$-4x - 200 = 0$

$+200\quad +200$

$-4x = 200$

$\dfrac{-4x}{-4} = \dfrac{200}{-4}$

$x = -50$

Because $x = -50$ is outside our domain and is not an allowable point for this problem, we disregard it. The derivative exists everywhere, and the endpoints are $x = 0$ and $x = 40$. Evaluating the function at $x = 0$ and $x = 40$, we have:

$x = 0,\ P(0) = -2(0)^2 - 200(0) - 900 = -\$900$

$x = 40, P(40) = -2(40)^2 - 200(40) - 900 = -3{,}200 - 8{,}000 - 900 = -\$12{,}000$

If the manufacturer produced 0 refrigerators, its max profit is a loss at $12,000

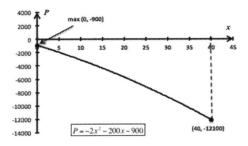

9. Marginal revenue is the derivative of the revenue.

   (a) $MR = R'(x) = 15$.

   (b) $MR = R'(x) = 200 - \dfrac{1}{4}(2x^{2-1}) = 200 - \dfrac{2}{4}x = 200 - \dfrac{1}{2}x$

   (c) $MR = R'(x) = 2.25 - 0.000025(2x^{2-1}) = 2.25 - 0.00005x$

11. Marginal cost is the derivative of cost:

   (a) $MC = C'(x) = \dfrac{1}{5{,}000}(2x^{2-1}) + 8 + 0 = \dfrac{2}{5{,}000}x + 8 = \dfrac{1}{2{,}500}x + 8$

   (b) $MC = C'(x) = 50 + 0 = 50$

   (c) $MC = C'(x) = 0 + 0.25 = 0.25$

13. Set $R'(x) = C'(x)$, where $R(x) = 200x$ and $C(x) = 5{,}000 + 20x + \dfrac{1}{2}x^2$, and solve for x.
   We have:

   $200 = 20 + x$

   $-20\quad -20$

   $180 = x$

Because $x = 180$ is outside our domain ($0 \le x \le 150$) and is not an allowable point for this problem, we disregard it. The derivative exists everywhere, and the endpoints are $x = 0$ and $x = 150$. Evaluating the function $P(x) = -\frac{1}{2}x^2 + 180x - 5,000$ at $x = 0$ and $x = 150$, we have:

$x = 0, P(0) = -\frac{1}{2}(0)^2 + 180(0) - 5,000 = -\$5,000$

$x = 150, P(150) = -\frac{1}{2}(150)^2 + 180(150) - 5,000 = \$10,750$

If the manufacturer produced 150 televisions, its profit will be $10,750.

15. $R'(x) = C'(x)$

$500 - 2(2x^{2-1}) = 300$

$500 - 4x = 300$

$\underline{-500 \qquad\quad -500}$

$-4x = -200$

$\dfrac{-4x}{-4} = \dfrac{-200}{-4}$

$x = 50$ Refrigerators

The derivative exists everywhere, and the endpoints are $x = 0$, $x = 50$ and $x = 100$. Evaluating the function at $x = 0$, $x = 50$, and $x = 100$, we have:

$x = 0, \ P(0) = -2(0)^2 + 200(0) - 2,000 = -\$2,000$

$x = 50, \ P(50) = -2(50)^2 + 200(50) - 2,000 = -5,000 + 10,000 - 2,000 = \$3,000$

$x = 100, \ P(100) = -2(100)^2 + 200(100) - 2,000 = -20,000 + 20,000 - 2,000$
$$= -\$2,000$$

The manufacturer should produce 50 refrigerators per week to have a maximum profit of $3,000.

Section 5.4: Minimizing Inventory Costs

1. $m = \$10, k = \$3$, and $D = 540$. The optimum order size (EOQ) $= x = \sqrt{\dfrac{2mD}{k}}$.

$EOQ = x = \sqrt{\dfrac{2(10)(540)}{3}} = \sqrt{\dfrac{10,800}{3}} = \sqrt{3,600} = 60$ items

3. Before we compute the optimum order size(EOQ), we must convert every parameter to yearly value. Using dimensional analysis, we have:

$k = \dfrac{\$2}{month} \cdot \dfrac{12 \ months}{1 \ year} = \$24$ per year.

The optimum order size (EOQ) $= x = \sqrt{\dfrac{2mD}{k}} = \sqrt{\dfrac{2(4.80)(1000)}{24}} = \sqrt{\dfrac{9,600}{24}} = \sqrt{400} = 20$

5. (a) $m = \$9.60, k = \$1.92$, and $D = 1,000$.

$$\text{The optimum order size (EOQ)} = \sqrt{\frac{2mD}{k}} = \sqrt{\frac{2(9.60)(1000)}{1.92}} = \sqrt{\frac{19,200}{1.92}}$$

$$= \sqrt{10,000} = 100 \text{ units}$$

(b) The number of orders placed in a year: $N = \dfrac{D}{x} = \dfrac{1000}{100} = 10$ orders per year.

7. (a) 800 appliances

(b) $N = \dfrac{D}{x} = \dfrac{2,400}{800} = 3$ orders per year.

(c) $D = N \cdot x = 3 \cdot 800 = 2,400$ appliances

9.

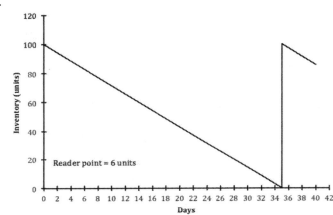

11. Differentiating $TC(x) = mDx^{-1} + \dfrac{k}{2}x$, for $1 \le x \le D$, we have:

$$TC'(x) = mD(-1x^{-1-1}) + \frac{k}{2} = -mDx^{-2} + \frac{k}{2}.$$

To locate all values of x for which the derivative is 0, we set the derivative to zero and solve for x. We have:

$$-mDx^{-2} + \frac{k}{2} = 0 \qquad\qquad 2 \cdot mD = \frac{kx^2}{2} \cdot 2$$

$$\frac{-mD}{x^2} + \frac{k}{2} = 0 \qquad\qquad 2mD = kx^2$$

$$\frac{-mD}{x^2} = -\frac{k}{2} \qquad\qquad \frac{2mD}{k} = \frac{kx^2}{k}$$

$$x^2 \cdot \frac{-mD}{x^2} = -\frac{k}{2} \cdot x^2 \qquad\qquad \frac{2mD}{k} = x^2$$

$$-mD = -\frac{kx^2}{2} \qquad\qquad x^2 = \frac{2mD}{k}$$

$$-(-mD) = -\left(-\frac{kx^2}{2}\right) \qquad\qquad x = \pm\sqrt{\frac{2mD}{k}}$$

Since the value of x is positive, $x = -\sqrt{\frac{2mD}{k}}$ is outside our domain and is not an

allowable point for this problem, we disregard it. The only solution is $x = \sqrt{\frac{2mD}{k}}$. Now,

we find the second derivative for the function $TC(x) = mDx^{-1} + \frac{k}{2}x$:

$$TC''(x) = \frac{d}{dx}\left(-mDx^{-2} + \frac{k}{2}\right) = -mD(-2x^{-2-1}) + 0 = 2mDx^{-3} = \frac{2mD}{x^3} > 0 \text{ for}$$

every x in [1, D]. For $x = \sqrt{\frac{2mD}{k}}$, $TC''\left(\sqrt{\frac{2mD}{k}}\right) = \frac{2mD}{\left(\sqrt{\frac{2mD}{k}}\right)^3}$. We see that $\frac{2mD}{\left(\sqrt{\frac{2mD}{k}}\right)^3} > 0$

because $2mD > 0$, $\sqrt{\frac{2mD}{k}} > 0$, and $\left(\sqrt{\frac{2mD}{k}}\right)^3 > 0$. Hence, $\frac{2mD}{\left(\sqrt{\frac{2mD}{k}}\right)^3} > 0$.

Therefore, by the second derivative test, $TC(x)$ achieves a relative minimum at $x = \sqrt{\frac{2mD}{k}}$.

Section 5.5: Econometrics

1. $\frac{dT}{dB} = \frac{1}{1-m} = \frac{1}{1-0.6} = \frac{1}{0.4} = 2.5 = \frac{2.5}{1}$. That is, T increases 2.5 units with every one-unit

change in B. A \$25 million change in B results in a theoretical change of $2.5 \cdot \$25\ million$ = \$62.5 $million$ in T.

3. With $T = C + B$ and $C = mT + C_0$, where C_0 is fixed, we can write a T as
$T = mT + C_0 + B$. Solving the resulting equation for T, we have:

$$T = mT + C_0 + B$$

$$-mT \quad - mT$$

$$T - mT = B + C_0$$

$$T(1 - m) = B + C_0$$

$$\frac{T(1-m)}{(1-m)} = \frac{B+C_0}{(1-m)}$$

$$T = \frac{B+C_0}{(1-m)} = \frac{B}{1-m} + \frac{C_0}{1-m} = \left(\frac{1}{1-m}\right)B + \frac{C_0}{1-m}$$

$$\frac{dT}{dB} = \frac{1}{1-m} + 0 = \frac{1}{1-m}$$

$\frac{dT}{dB} = \frac{1}{1-m} = \frac{1}{1-0.6} = \frac{1}{0.4} = 2.5 = \frac{2.5}{1}$. That is, T increases 2.5 units with every

one-unit change in B. A \$25 million change in B results in a theoretical change of

$2.5 \cdot \$25 \ million = \$62.5 \ million$ in T.

5. \$2,383.36 increase

Chapter 6 Curve Fitting and Trend Lines

Section 6.1: Constant Curve Fit

1. $y = \dfrac{12+13+9+8+11+10+9+13+8+10}{10} = \dfrac{103}{10} = 10.3$

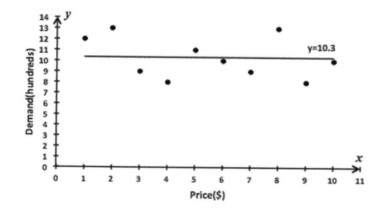

3. $y = \dfrac{28+29+32+27+26+31+28+27+30}{9} = \dfrac{258}{9} = 28.7$

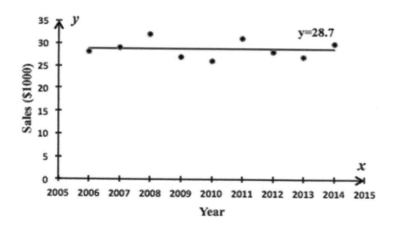

5. An increase does not seem advisable, as sales appear to decrease as advertising is increased. (In Section 6.2, the average rate of change of sales with respect to advertising can be determined, which will show that sales do, in fact, decrease with an increase in advertising—see the solution to Exercise 1 in Section 6.2.)

Section 6.2: Linear Least-Squares Trend Lines

1. (Exercise 5, Page 141)

TABLE 6.4

Year	2006	2007	2008	2009	2010	2011	2012	2013	2014
Advertising ($1,000)	140	150	160	170	180	160	160	170	170
Sales	28	29	32	26	26	27	28	27	30

To find the least-squares straight line ($y = mx + b$) for the data in TABLE 6.4, we need to solve the system of equations:

(1) $\quad bN + m\sum_{i=1}^{N} x_i = \sum_{i=1}^{N} y_i$

(2) $\quad b\sum_{i=1}^{N} x_i + m\sum_{i=1}^{N} (x_i)^2 = \sum_{i=1}^{N} (x_i y_i)$

A good procedure for calculating the least-squares straight line is to first construct table for the values in the equations (1) and (2). We have:

x_i	y_i	$(x_i)^2$	$x_i y_i$
140	28	19,600	3,920
150	29	22,500	4,350
160	32	25,600	5,120
170	26	28,900	4,420
180	26	32,400	4,680
160	27	25,600	4,320
160	28	25,600	4,480
170	27	28,900	4,590
170	30	28,900	5,100
$\sum_{i=1}^{9} x_i = 1,460$	$\sum_{i=1}^{9} y_i = 253$	$\sum_{i=1}^{9} (x_i)^2 = 238,000$	$\sum_{i=1}^{9} (x_i y_i) = 40,980$

Equations (1) and (2) become:

(1) $9b + 1460m = 253$
(2) $1460b + 238,000m = 40,980$

Using the Elimination Method, we will remove b by multiplying equation (1) by $-1,460$ and equation (2) by 9. We have:

(1) $-1,460(9b + 1,460m = 253) \quad \leftrightarrow -13,140b - 2,131,600m = -369,380$
(2) $9(1,460b + 238,000m = 40,980) \leftrightarrow \quad 13,140b + 2,142,000m = 368,820$

Add equations (1) and (2). The resulting equation is $10,400m = -560$. Solving the equation for

m, we have $m = \frac{-560}{10,400} = -0.0538$. To find b, we substitute $m = -0.0538$ into either equation (1) or (2). Either equations will result in the same b. So, let's choose equation (1). We have:

$9b + 1460m = 253$

$9b + 1460(-0.0538) = 253$

$9b - 78.548 = 253$

$+78.548 \quad + 78.548$

$9b = 331.548$

$\frac{9b}{9} = \frac{331.548}{9}$

$b = 36.839$

Therefore, the least-squares straight line is $y = -0.0538x + 36.839$, where y represents Sales and x represents Advertising Budget. Because sales go down (The slope $m = -0.0538$ is negative) as advertising increased, it does not make sense to increase the advertising budget (See Figure 1)

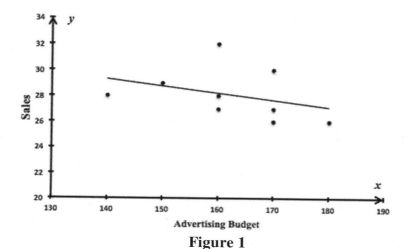

Figure 1

3. (a)

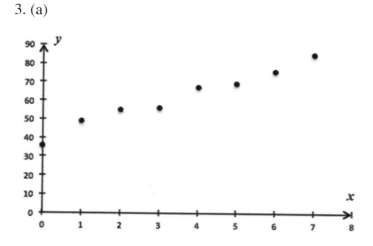

Yes. A straight-line approximation for the trend seems quite reasonable. We see that as the value of x increases, y also increases.

(b)

x	0	1	2	3	4	5	6	7
y	36	49	55	56	67	69	76	85

To find the least-squares straight line ($y = mx + b$) for the data, we need to solve the system of equations:

(1) $\quad bN + m\sum_{i=1}^{N} x_i = \sum_{i=1}^{N} y_i$

(2) $\quad b\sum_{i=1}^{N} x_i + m\sum_{i=1}^{N} (x_i)^2 = \sum_{i=1}^{N} (x_i y_i)$

A good procedure for calculating the least-squares straight line is to first construct table for the values in the equations (1) and (2).

We have:

x_i	y_i	$(x_i)^2$	$x_i y_i$
0	36	0	0
1	49	1	49
2	55	4	110
3	56	9	168
4	67	16	268
5	69	25	345
6	76	36	456
7	85	49	595
$\sum_{i=1}^{8} x_i = 28$	$\sum_{i=1}^{8} y_i = 493$	$\sum_{i=1}^{8} (x_i)^2 = 140$	$\sum_{i=1}^{8} (x_i y_i) = 1{,}991$

Equations (1) and (2) become:

(3) $8b + 28m = 493$
(4) $28b + 140m = 1{,}991$

Using the Elimination Method, we will remove b by multiplying equation (1) by -28 and equation (2) by 8. We have:

(1) $-28(8b + 28m = 493) \quad \leftrightarrow -224b - 784m = -13{,}804$
(2) $8(28b + 140m = 1{,}991) \quad \leftrightarrow \quad 224b + 1{,}120m = 15{,}928$

Add equations (1) and (2). The resulting equation is $336m = 2{,}124$. Solving the equation for m, we have $m = \frac{2{,}124}{336} = 6.321$. To find b, we substitute $m = 6.321$ into either equation (1) or (2). Either equation will result with the same b. So, let's choose equation (1). We have:

$8b + 28m = 493$

$8b + 28(6.321) = 493$

$$8b + 176.988 = 493$$

$$-176.988 \quad -176.988$$

$$8b = 316.012$$

$$\frac{8b}{8} = \frac{316.012}{8}$$

$$b = 39.502$$

Therefore, the least-squares straight line is $y = 6.321x + 39.502$.

(c)

Given Data		Evaluated
x	y	$y = 6.321x + 39.502$
0	36	$6.321(0) + 39.502 = 39.502$
1	49	$6.321(1) + 39.502 = 45.823$
2	55	$6.321(2) + 39.502 = 52.144$
3	56	$6.321(3) + 39.502 = 58.465$
4	67	$6.321(4) + 39.502 = 64.786$
5	69	$6.321(5) + 39.502 = 71.107$
6	76	$6.321(6) + 39.502 = 77.428$
7	85	$6.321(7) + 39.502 = 83.749$

$$e(0) = 36 - 39.502 = -3.502$$
$$e(1) = 49 - 45.823 = 3.177$$
$$e(2) = 55 - 52.144 = 2.856$$
$$e(3) = 56 - 58.465 = -2.465$$
$$e(4) = 67 - 64.786 = 2.214$$
$$e(5) = 69 - 71.107 = -2.107$$
$$e(6) = 76 - 77.428 = -1.428$$
$$e(7) = 85 - 83.749 = 1.251$$

The least-squares error:

$$E = [e(0)]^2 + [e(1)]^2 + [e(2)]^2 + [e(3)]^2 + [e(4)]^2 + [e(5)]^2 + [e(6)]^2 + [e(7)]^2$$

$$= (-3.502)^2 + (3.177)^2 + (2.856)^2 + (-2.465)^2 + (2.214)^2 + (-2.107)^2 + (-1.428)^2 + (1.251)^2$$

$$= 49.536$$

(d)

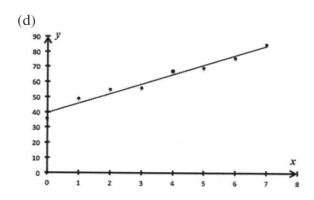

5. (a) Let 1 represent the year 2007, 2 for 2008, 3 for 2009, etc. TABLE 6.14 becomes:

Year	1	2	3	4	5	6	7
Sales(thousands)	15	18	16	20	18	22	19

To find the least-squares straight line ($y = mx + b$) for the data, we need to solve the system of equations:

(1) $\quad bN + m\sum_{i=1}^{N} x_i = \sum_{i=1}^{N} y_i$

(2) $\quad b\sum_{i=1}^{N} x_i + m\sum_{i=1}^{N} (x_i)^2 = \sum_{i=1}^{N} (x_i y_i)$

A good procedure for calculating the least-squares straight line is to first construct table for the values in the equations (1) and (2).

We have:

x_i	y_i	$(x_i)^2$	$x_i y_i$
1	15	1	15
2	18	4	36
3	16	9	48
4	20	16	80
5	18	25	90
6	22	36	132
7	19	49	133
$\sum_{i=1}^{7} x_i = 28$	$\sum_{i=1}^{7} y_i = 128$	$\sum_{i=1}^{7} (x_i)^2 = 140$	$\sum_{i=1}^{7} (x_i y_i) = 534$

Equations (1) and (2) become:

(1) $7b + 28m = 128$
(2) $28b + 140m = 534$

Using the Elimination Method, we will remove b by multiplying equation (1) by -28 and equation (2) by 7. We have:

(1) $-28(7b + 28m = 128) \leftrightarrow -196b - 784m = -3{,}584$
(2) $7(28b + 140m = 534) \leftrightarrow 196b + 980m = 3{,}738$

Add equations (1) and (2). The resulting equation is $196m = 154$. Solving the equation for m, we have: $m = \frac{154}{195} = 0.786$. To find b, we substitute $m = 0.786$ into either equation (1) or (2). Either equation will result with the same b. So, let's choose equation (1). We have:

$7b + 28m = 128$

$7b + 28(0.786) = 128$

$7b + 22.008 = 128$

$\underline{-22.008 \quad -22.008}$

$7b = 105.992$

$\dfrac{7b}{7} = \dfrac{105.992}{7}$

$b = 15.142$

Therefore, the least-squares straight line is $y = 0.786x + 15.142$, where y represents Sales and x represents year.

(b) The year 2011 is represented by $x = 5$.

Therefore, Sales $= y = 0.786(5) + 15.142 = \$19.072$ thousands or $19,072.

(c) The year 2018 is represented by $x = 12$.

Therefore, Sales $= y = 0.786(12) + 15.142 = 24.574$ thousands or $24,574.

7.

TABLE 6.16

Rain (inches)	2.0	2.2	2.3	3.2	3.8	4.9	5.6
Yield (bushels)	25	25	30	30	40	50	50

To find the least-squares straight line ($y = mx + b$) for the data, we need to solve the system of equations:

(1) $$bN + m\sum_{i=1}^{N} x_i = \sum_{i=1}^{N} y_i$$

(2) $$b\sum_{i=1}^{N} x_i + m\sum_{i=1}^{N}(x_i)^2 = \sum_{i=1}^{N}(x_i y_i)$$

A good procedure for calculating the least-squares straight line is to first construct table for the values in the equations (1) and (2). We have:

x_i	y_i	$(x_i)^2$	$x_i y_i$
2.0	25	4	50
2.2	25	4.84	55
2.3	30	5.29	69
3.2	30	10.24	96
3.8	40	14.44	152
4.9	50	24.01	245
5.6	50	31.36	280
$\sum_{i=1}^{7} x_i = 24$	$\sum_{i=1}^{7} y_i = 250$	$\sum_{i=1}^{7}(x_i)^2 = 94.18$	$\sum_{i=1}^{7}(x_i y_i) = 947$

Equations (1) and (2) become:

(1) $7b + 24m = 250$
(2) $24b + 94.18m = 947$

Using the Elimination Method, we will remove b by multiplying equation (1) by -24 and equation (2) by 7. We have:

(1) $-24(7b + 24m = 250)$ $\leftrightarrow$ $-168b - 576m = -6,000$
(2) $7(24b + 94.18m = 947)$ $\leftrightarrow$ $168b + 659.26m = 6,629$

Add equations (1) and (2). The resulting equation is $83.26m = 629$. Solving the equation for m, we have $m = \frac{629}{83.26} = 7.555$. To find b, we substitute $m = 7.5546$ into either equation (1) or (2). Either equation will result with the same b. So, let's choose equation (1).

We have:

$7b + 24m = 250$

$7b + 24(7.5546) = 250$

$7b + 181.3104 = 250$

$\quad -181.3104 \quad -181.3104$

$7b = 68.6896$

$\dfrac{7b}{7} = \dfrac{68.6896}{7}$

$b = 9.8128$

Therefore, the least-squares straight line is $y = 7.5546x + 9.8128$, where y represent Yield and x represent inches of rain.

For $x = 3.5$, Yield $= y = 7.5546(3.5) + 9.8128 = 36.2539$.

Section 6.3: Quadratic and Exponential Trend Lines

1. By hand calculations:

TABLE 6.22

x	0	1	2	3	4
y	10	11	15	16	23

<u>Algebraically</u>

To find the least-squares quadratic trend line ($y = ax^2 + bx + c$) for the data, we need to solve the system of equations:

$$(1) \quad cN + b\sum_{i=1}^{N} x_i + a\sum_{i=1}^{N} (x_i)^2 = \sum_{i=1}^{N} y_i$$

$$(2) \quad c\sum_{i=1}^{N} x_i + b\sum_{i=1}^{N} (x_i)^2 + a\sum_{i=1}^{N} (x_i)^3 = \sum_{i=1}^{N} (x_i y_i)$$

$$(3) \quad c\sum_{i=1}^{N} (x_i)^2 + b\sum_{i=1}^{N} (x_i)^3 + a\sum_{i=1}^{N} (x_i)^4 = \sum_{i=1}^{N} (x_i)^2 y_i$$

A good procedure for calculating the least-squares quadratic trend line is to first construct table for the values in the equations (1), (2), and (3). We have:

x_i	y_i	$(x_i)^2$	$(x_i)^3$	$(x_i)^4$	$x_i y_i$	$(x_i)^2 y_i$
0	10	0	0	0	0	0
1	11	1	1	1	11	11
2	15	4	8	16	30	60
3	16	9	27	81	48	144
4	23	16	64	256	92	368
SUM=10	SUM=75	SUM=30	SUM=100	SUM=354	SUM=181	SUM=583

Equations (1), (2), and (3) become:

(1) $5c + 10b + 30a = 75$

(2) $10c + 30b + 100a = 181$

(3) $30c + 100b + 354a = 583$

To solve a system of three equations with three variables, the objective is to reduce it to a system of two equations with two variables by eliminating one variable of your choosing. Then, reduce the system of two equations with two variables to one equation with one variable. After that, back substitute to find the other two missing variables.

STEP 1: Using the Additive Method (Elimination), choose to remove c by combining any two equations from the three. This in turn will create a system of two equations with two variables. Let's combine equations (1) and (2) and (1) and (3).
Eliminate c by multiplying equation (1) by -10 and equation (2) by 5.

(1) $5c + 10b + 30a = 75$ $\quad\leftrightarrow\quad -10(5c + 10b + 30a = 75)$
(2) $10c + 30b + 100a = 181$ $\leftrightarrow\quad 5(10c + 30b + 100a = 181)$

$\leftrightarrow -50c - 100b - 300a = -750$
$\leftrightarrow \quad 50c + 150b + 500a = 905$

Add equations (1) and (2). The resulting equation is $50b + 200a = 155$. Let's call this new equation (A).

STEP 2: Repeat this procedure for equations (1) and (3). Eliminate c by multiplying equation (1) by -30 and equation (3) by 5.

(1) $5c + 10b + 30a = 75$ $\quad\leftrightarrow\quad -30(5c + 10b + 30a = 75)$
(3) $30c + 100b + 354a = 583$ $\leftrightarrow\quad 5(30c + 100b + 354a = 583)$

$\leftrightarrow -150c - 300b - 900a = -2,250$
$\leftrightarrow \quad 150c + 500b + 1,770a = 2,915$

Add equations (1) and (3). The resulting equation is $200b + 870a = 665$. Let's call this new equation (B).

STEP 3: We now have a system of two equations with two variables.

(A) $50b + 200a = 155$
(B) $200b + 870a = 665$

Using the Addition Method, reduce this system of two equations with two variables to one equation with one variable. Once again, choose either b or a to eliminate. Let's choose to eliminate b by multiplying equation (A) by -200 and equation (B) by 50.

(A) $50b + 200a = 155$ ↔ $-200(50b + 200a = 155)$
(B) $200b + 870a = 655$ ↔ $50(200b + 870a = 665)$

↔ $-10,000b - 40,000a = -31,000$
↔ $10,000b + 43,500a = 33,250$

Add equations (A) and (B). The resulting equation is $3,500a = 2,250$. Solving the equation for a, we have $a = \frac{2,250}{3,500} = 0.643$. To find b, we substitute $a = 0.643$ into either equation (A) or (B). Either equation will result with the same b. So, let's choose equation (A). We have:

$50b + 200a = 155$

$50b + 200(0.643) = 155$

$50b + 128.60 = 155$
$\quad -128.60 \qquad -128.60$

$50b = 26.40$

$\dfrac{50b}{50} = \dfrac{26.40}{50}$

$b = 0.528$

STEP 4: Lastly, we need to find c by substituting the values for a and b into either equation (1), (2), or (3). The same c will be achieved no matter which equation is used. Let's choose equation (1). We have:
$5c + 10b + 30a = 7$

$5c + 10(0.528) + 30(0.643) = 75$ $\qquad$ $5c = 50.43$

$5c + 5.28 + 19.29 = 75$ $\qquad$ $\dfrac{5c}{5} = \dfrac{50.43}{5}$

$5c + 24.57 = 75$ $\qquad$ $c = 10.086$

$\quad -24.57 \qquad -24.57$

The least-squares quadratic trend line is $y = 0.643x^2 + 0.528x + 10.086$.

By using Excel, we obtain the following graph and its equation:

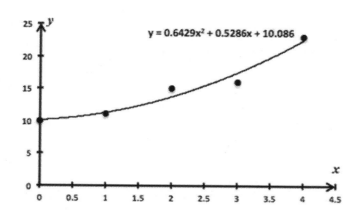

$$y = 0.6429x^2 + 0.5286x + 10.086$$

3. **PART 1:** To find the least-squares straight line ($y = mx + b$) for the data, we need to solve the system of equations:

$$(1) \quad bN + m\sum_{i=1}^{N} x_i = \sum_{i=1}^{N} y_i$$

$$(2) \quad b\sum_{i=1}^{N} x_i + m\sum_{i=1}^{N} (x_i)^2 = \sum_{i=1}^{N} (x_i y_i)$$

A good procedure for calculating the least-squares straight line is to first construct table for the values in the equations (1) and (2). Equations (1) and (2) become:

(1) $5b + 10m = 75$
(2) $10b + 30m = 181$

Using the Elimination Method, we will remove b by multiplying equation (1) by -10 and equation (2) by 5. We have:

(1) $-10(5b + 10m = 75) \leftrightarrow -50b - 100m = -750$
(2) $5(10b + 30m = 181) \leftrightarrow 50b + 150m = 905$

Add equations (1) and (2). The resulting equation is $50m = 155$. Solving the equation for m, we have $m = \frac{155}{50} = 3.1$. To find b, we substitute $m = 3.1$ into either equation (1) or (2). Either equation will result with the same b. So, let's choose equation (1). We have:

$5b + 10m = 75$

$5b + 10(3.1) = 75$

$5b + 31 = 75$

$-31 \quad -31$

$5b = 44$

$\dfrac{5b}{5} = \dfrac{44}{5}$

$b = 8.8$

Therefore, the least-squares straight line is $y = 3.1x + 8.8$.

PART 2: Least-squares straight line error.

$x = 0, y = 3.1(0) + 8.8 = 8.8$
$x = 1, y = 3.1(1) + 8.8 = 11.9$
$x = 2, y = 3.1(2) + 8.8 = 15$
$x = 3, y = 3.1(3) + 8.8 = 18.1$
$x = 4, y = 3.1(4) + 8.8 = 21.2$

The least-squares straight line error:

$$E_s = [e(0)]^2 + [e(1)]^2 + [e(2)]^2 + [e(3)]^2 + [e(4)]^2$$

$$= (1.2)^2 + (-.9)^2 + (0)^2 + (-2.1)^2 + (1.8)^2 = 9.9$$

PART 3: The least-squares quadratic trend line error.

$x = 0, y = 0.643(0)^2 + 0.528(0) + 10.086 = 10.086$

$x = 1, y = 0.643(1)^2 + 0.528(1) + 10.086 = 11.257$

$x = 2, y = 0.643(2)^2 + 0.528(2) + 10.086 = 13.714$

$x = 3, y = 0.643(3)^2 + 0.528(3) + 10.086 = 17.457$

$x = 4, y = 0.643(4)^2 + 0.528(4) + 10.086 = 22.486$

The least-squares quadratic trend line error:

$$E_Q = [e(0)]^2 + [e(1)]^2 + [e(2)]^2 + [e(3)]^2 + [e(4)]^2$$

$$= (-.086)^2 + (-.257)^2 + (1.286)^2 + (-1.457)^2 + (.514)^2 = 4.11$$

The least-squares quadratic trend line has smaller error than the least-squares straight line.
PART 4:

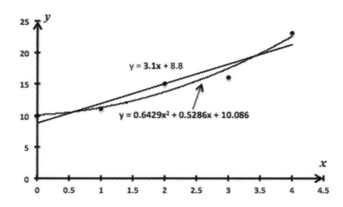

5.

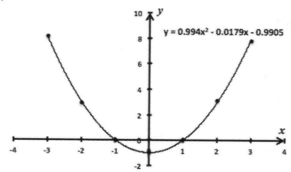

$y = 0.994x^2 - 0.0179x - 0.9905$

7. (a) **Calculating by hand.**

x	-1	0	1
y	0	7	10

To find the three simultaneous equations below, we need to find all the sums involved.

(1) $\quad cN + b\sum_{i=1}^{N} x_i + a\sum_{i=1}^{N}(x_i)^2 = \sum_{i=1}^{N} y_i$

(2) $\quad c\sum_{i=1}^{N} x_i + b\sum_{i=1}^{N}(x_i)^2 + a\sum_{i=1}^{N}(x_i)^3 = \sum_{i=1}^{N}(x_i y_i)$

(3) $\quad c\sum_{i=1}^{N}(x_i)^2 + b\sum_{i=1}^{N}(x_i)^3 + a\sum_{i=1}^{N}(x_i)^4 = \sum_{i=1}^{N}(x_i)^2 y_i$

Construct a table for the values in the equations (1), (2), and (3). We have:

x_i	y_i	$(x_i)^2$	$(x_i)^3$	$(x_i)^4$	$x_i y_i$	$(x_i)^2 y_i$
-1	0	1	-1	1	0	0
0	7	0	0	0	0	0
1	10	1	1	1	10	10
SUM =0	SUM= 17	SUM = 2	SUM= 0	SUM=2	SUM=10	SUM=10

Equations (1), (2), and (3) become:

(1) $3c + 0b + 2a = 17 \quad \leftrightarrow \quad 3c + 2a = 17$

(2) $0c + 2b + 0a = 10 \quad \leftrightarrow \quad 2b = 10$

(3) $2c + 0b + 2a = 10 \quad \leftrightarrow \quad 2c + 2a = 10$

(b) To solve a system of three equations with three variables, the objective is to reduce it to a system of two equations with two variables by eliminating one variable of your choosing. Then, reduce the system of two equations with two variables to one equation with one variable. After that, back substitute to find the other two missing variables.

Equation (2) can be solved immediately for b. $b = \frac{10}{2} = 5$. We are now left with only with the values of a and c to find. Using equations (1) and (3), we will be able to determine the values.

Using the Additive Method (Elimination), choose to remove c by multiplying equation (1) by -2 and equation (3) by 3. We have:

(1) $3c + 2a = 17 \leftrightarrow -2(3c + 2a = 17) \leftrightarrow -6c - 4a = -34$
(3) $2c + 2a = 10 \leftrightarrow 3(2c + 2a = 10) \quad \leftrightarrow 6c + 6a = 30$

Add equations (1) and (3). The resulting equation is $2a = -4$. Solving for a, we have:

$a = \frac{-4}{2} = -2$. To find c, we substitute $a = -2$ into either equation (1) or (3). Either equation will results with the same b. So, let's choose equation (1). We have:

$3c + 2a = 17$ $3c = 21$

$3c + 2(-2) = 17$ $\frac{3c}{3} = \frac{21}{3}$

$3c - 4 = 17$

$\quad +4 \quad +4$ $c = 7$

Therefore, $a = -2, b = 5$, and $c = 7$.

9.

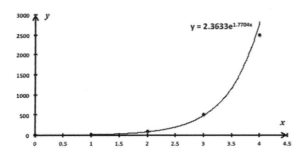

11. (a)

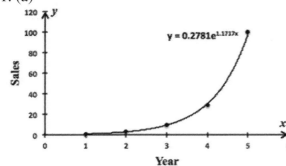

(b) Note: Assuming that 1 represent the year 2001, 2 represent the year 2002, etc.

For $x = 16$, $Sales = y = 0.2781e^{1.1717(16)} = \$38,548,412.71$

Workbook

CHAPTER 1

For 1 – 22, evaluate the following expressions. Remember to reduce every fraction in the final answer.

1. $18 + (-6)$

2. $-10 + 6$

3. $21.9 + (4.7)$

4. $44 - (-18)$

5. $-7 - 8$

6. $15 - 4$

7. $3(-7)$

8. $-8(6)$

9. $(-2.1)(-5.1)$

10. $9\left(-\frac{1}{2}\right)$

11. $-12 - (-9)$

12. $\frac{-16}{2}$

13. $\frac{81}{-3}$

14. $\frac{-21}{-7}$

15. $\frac{12}{25} \cdot \left(-\frac{3}{4}\right)$

16. $[5(-2) + 7(4)]$

17. $\left(-\frac{5}{12}\right) \cdot \left(-\frac{4}{15}\right)$

18. $\frac{14+7}{6-3}$

19. $\{2[5(1.7) - 6(-3.2)] - 1\}$

20. $\frac{\frac{[18-28]}{5} + 7(2-6)}{5[-4-(-16)]}$

21. $\frac{9[3(2)-5(-1)]-6[11-4)]}{5}$

22. $\frac{3[-2(7-4)-9(11-8)]}{6[5(4-1)+10(2-8)]}$

For 23 – 27, determine whether or not the proposed values of the unknowns are solutions of the given systems.

23. $3x - 7 = 5;$ $\qquad x = 7.$

24. $9y + 14 = 8y;$ $\qquad y = -14.$

25. $6(p + 9) = 4 - 2(p - 1);$ $\qquad p = -6.$

26. $\frac{(w+1)(w-2)}{2w-1} = w + 1;$ $\qquad w = 1.$

27. $\frac{(3m+1)(m-1)-12}{2(m-3)+1} = m + 3;$ $\qquad m = 2.$

28. Determine whether or not $x = 2$ is a solution of the following equation if it is known that $y = -3$ and $z = 1$.

$$\frac{5(x+y)-xz}{y(z-x)} = \frac{3x+z}{y}$$

For 29 – 39, solve each equation for the unknown quantity.

29. $x + 9 = 14$

30. $2y - 3 = y + 7$

31. $-3p = 15$

32. $\frac{2}{3}m = -16$

33. $3(g - 2) + 7 = 1 - 5g$

34. $6 - 2(x + 1) = 10x$

35. $\frac{t+7}{9} = \frac{4t-3}{2}$

36. $\frac{4(1-3y)+15}{16} = 7y + 1$

37. $\frac{3}{7}x + \frac{5}{2} = \frac{1x}{3} - \frac{2}{7}$

38. $\frac{1-9(k+2)+6(k-1)}{4(k-7)-2(k+2)} = 10$

39. $\frac{z-7}{2} = \frac{3z+10}{3} + 1$

For 40 – 48, simplify each of the given expressions into one exponent. Make sure that each solution is given with a positive exponent.

40. $\frac{2^5 2^3}{2^2 2}$

41. $\frac{5^7 5^{-3} 5^2}{5^4 5^{-2}}$

42. $\frac{x^{11}x^{-13}x}{x^{-7}x^2 x^3}$

43. $\frac{(2.1)^3(2.1)^{-6}(2.1)^4}{(2.1)^8(2.1)^{-1}(2.1)^{-5}}$

44. $\frac{(y^3)^{-2}(y^{-5})^2 y^7}{(y^{-2})^4(y^{-2})^{-4}}$

45. $\pi^3(\pi^{-2})^7 \pi^8$

46. $\left(\frac{1}{3}\right)^7 \cdot \left(\frac{1}{3}\right)^{-8} \cdot \left(\frac{1}{3}\right)^4$

47. $\left[\left(-\frac{3}{4}\right)^2\right]^{-3} \left[\left(-\frac{3}{4}\right)^{-1}\right]^{-4} \left[\left(-\frac{3}{4}\right)^5\right]^2$

48. $\{[(4.5)^3]^{-2}\}^{-5}$

Using a calculator, determine the exact values of the qualities given in 49 – 59.

49. $4^{5/2}$

50. $25^{-3/2}$

51. $8^{2/3}$

52. $(-27)^{-4/3}$

53. $(12)^{1/2}(3^{3/2})$

54. $(2)^{3/2}(50)^{1/2}$

55. $(7)^{-2/3}(56)^{1/3}$

56. $\sqrt{\frac{4}{9}}$

57. $\sqrt{\frac{50}{8}}$

58. $\sqrt[3]{\frac{16}{54}}$

59. $\sqrt[4]{\frac{(16)(4)}{625}}$

For 60 – 76, solve the following equations for the unknown quantity (note: factoring can be used whenever it is appropriate). No rounding.

60. $x^2 = 4$

61. $y^3 = -27$

62. $p^6 = 64$

63. $m^4 = 16$

64. $w^{-2} = \frac{1}{25}$

65. $x^3 = 2$

66. $y^{2.1} = 7$

67. $z^{-1.9} = 15$

68. $x^9 = \pi$

69. $x^2 + 3x + 2 = 0$ 70. $y^2 - 2y + 1 = 0$ 71. $2n^2 - n = 3$

72. $3z^2 - 9z = 0$ 73. $3c^2 + 6c - 24 = 0$ 74. $9x = x^2 + 1$

75. $3y^2 - 10y = 8$ 76. $p^2 - p + 2 = 0$

For 77 – 82, plot each of the following points on the same coordinate system:

77. $(2, 0)$ 78. $(3, 5)$ 79. $(-4, -7)$

80. $(-6, 9)$ 81. $(0, -10)$ 82. $(8, -3)$

83. Consider the points labeled A through J in **Figure 1**.

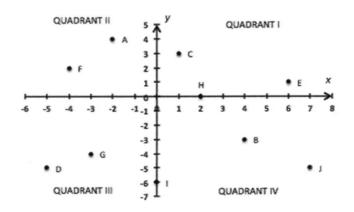

Figure 1

    a. Determine the coordinates of each point.

    b. Which point is located in Quadrant III?

84. a. Determine the value of the x-component of every point on the y-axis.

    b. Determine the value of the y-component of every point on the x-axis.

85. Construct a Cartesian coordinate system and draw a line parallel to the y-axis. What do all the points on this line have in common?

For 86 – 98, plot the graphs of the equations.

86. $3x - 5y = 15$ 87. $y = 2x - 1$ 88. $y - x = 0$

89. $6y - 7x = -42$ 90. $y - x^2 = 0$ 91. $y = \frac{3}{2}x + 1$

92. $y = -x^2$ 93. $y = x^2 - 2x + 1$ 94. $y = x^3$

95. $y = -x^3$ 96. $y = -\sqrt{x}$ 97. $y = x^3 - 5x^2 - x$

98. $x^2 + y^2 = 0$

99. Graph the two equations $y = 2x - 1$ and $y = 4x + 7$ on the same coordinate system. Determine the point of intersection of these curves from the resulting graph.

100. Graphically show that the two equations $y = x^2 - 1$ and $y = x^2$ have no points in common.

101. Determine if the points having coordinates $(0, -7)$, $(-1, 0)$, and $(3, 32)$ lie on the graph of the equation $y = 5x^2 - 2x - 7$.

For 102 – 108, write the expanded form of the following expressions:

102. $\sum_{i=1}^{4} (x^i)^2$

103. $\sum_{k=2}^{5} (6y_k)$

104. $\sum_{j=1}^{4} (2\sqrt{j})$

105. $\sum_{i=1}^{6} 9$

106. $\sum_{m=1}^{7} (x_m + y_m)$

107. $\sum_{n=0}^{3} (x_n y_n)$

108. $\sum_{i=1}^{4} (x_i) - \sum_{i=1}^{4} (y_i)$

For 109 – 116, write the expanded form of the following expressions:

109. $\sum_{i=1}^{8} i$

110. $\sum_{k=1}^{6} \left(\frac{k}{k+1} \right)$

111. $\sum_{j=0}^{7} (j-4)$

112. $\sum_{m=1}^{5} \left[(-1)^m m \right]$

113. $\sum_{p=1}^{10} (p-5)^2$

114. $\sum_{m=1}^{5} 3$

115. $\sum_{i=1}^{8} \left(\frac{i-1}{i+1} \right)$

116. $\sum_{h=1}^{9} i\sqrt{i+1}$

For 117 – 122, write the following expressions in sigma notation.

117. $-1 + 2 - 3 + 4 - 5 + 6$

118. $3(1)^1 + 3(2)^2 + 3(3)^3 + 3(4)^4 + 3(5)^5$

119. $1 + \frac{1}{2} + \frac{1}{3} + \cdots + \frac{1}{100}$

120. $5\sqrt{1} + 5\sqrt{2} + 5\sqrt{3} + 5\sqrt{4} + 5\sqrt{5} + 5\sqrt{6}$

121. $-\frac{2}{3} + \frac{3}{4} - \frac{4}{5} + \frac{5}{6} - \frac{6}{7} + \frac{7}{8}$

122. $\left(\frac{1}{2}\right)^2 + \left(\frac{2}{3}\right)^2 + \left(\frac{3}{4}\right)^2 + \cdots + \left(\frac{49}{50}\right)^2$

For 123 – 130, calculate the following sums for the data given in **Table 1**.

Table 1

k	x	y
1	0	5
2	1	−1
3	2	8
4	−1	3
5	−2	6
6	−3	10

123. $\displaystyle\sum_{i=1}^{4} x_i$

124. $\displaystyle\sum_{j=1}^{6} y_j$

125. $\displaystyle\sum_{m=1}^{5}(x_m - y_m)$

126. $\displaystyle\sum_{k=2}^{6}(2x_k y_k)$

127. $\displaystyle\sum_{p=1}^{6}\left(\frac{x_p}{y_p}\right)$

128. $\displaystyle\sum_{i=3}^{6}(y_i - x_i)$

129. $\displaystyle\sum_{n=1}^{6}(x_n)^2 + \sum_{n=1}^{6}(y_n)^2$

130. Show that $\displaystyle\sum_{i=1}^{n}(x_i - y_i) = \sum_{i=1}^{n} x_i - \sum_{i=1}^{n} y_i$.

For 131 – 135, use a calculator to find the equivalent decimal values for the given fractions, and then round (that is, use arithmetic rounding) the number to two decimal places.

131. $\dfrac{1}{6}$

132. $\dfrac{31}{25}$

133. $\dfrac{21}{13}$

134. $\dfrac{6}{7}$

135. $\dfrac{5}{9}$

136. Repeat Problems 131 – 135 and round the number to three decimal places.

For 137 – 142, convert the numbers written in exponential notation to standard decimal numbers.

137. 2.038749 E3

138. 3.1200956 E7

139. 1.927 E10

140. 9.20487 E–2

141. 6.00143 E–9

142. 5.71 E–4

CHAPTER 2

1. Determine which of the following equations are linear.

   a. $3y = 5x$

   b. $y - x = 0$

   c. $x = \sqrt{y}$

   d. $y + 7 = 4x$

   e. $7xy = 4$

   f. $y^{1/2} + x^{1/2} = 9$

   g. $\dfrac{3}{x} - \dfrac{4}{y} = 1$

   h. $y = 9x^2$

   i. $x + 9 = 4$

   j. $y - 7 = 0$

   k. $-2x + 9y = 0$

   l. $x^2 + y^2 = 1$

2. An appliance salesperson working for a high-end department store determines that the number of each appliance sold, denoted by x, is directly related to the income earned each year, denoted by y. Her base salary is $35,000 and, for each appliance she sold, she will earn a commission of $250.

   a. Determine the equation relating x to y and show that this equation is linear.

   b. What would be the salesperson's income if she sold 69 appliances by the end of year?

   c. How many appliances would the salesperson need to sell to earn a $75,000 income?

3. After extensive researches for a motorcycle, Gary bought a high-end motorcycle from a friend's dealership that cost him $15,000. He decides to trade it in for a new model at the end of two years. His friend quoted the depreciation rate as 12% per year. Let y denote the value of Gary's motorcycle at any given time and let t denote time measure in year.

   a. Determine the equation relating t to the y and show that it is a linear equation.

   b. Find the value of Gary's motorcycle after one and a half year later.

4. The Jones's family grocery expenditure is defined by the equation $E = 5.75x + 250$, where the number of weeks is denoted by x, and the total expenditure is denoted by E.

   (a) Find the Jones's grocery expenditure for three weeks.

   (b) How many weeks will it take the Jones to spend $500 in grocery?

5. Graph the following equations:

   a. $5x - 2y = 10$

   b. $-4x + 3y = 12$

   c. $-7x - 2y = 14$

   d. $y = \dfrac{1}{2}x + 1$

   e. $y - 3 = 2$

   f. $0.5x + 2.5y = 25$

   g. $4N + 5M = -20$

   h. $-2D + P = 4$

   i. $C - 3x = 9$

   j. $R = \dfrac{2}{3}C$

   k. $5S - 3D = 15$

   l. $x + 9 = 0$

6. Pete's Steak House monthly profits (in thousands of dollars) are given by $P = 900N - 750$, where N represents the number of months and P represents the monthly profit. Determine the number of months that it will take for the restaurant to make $590,000.

7. Benjamin is going to college and needs a new computer. Through his research, he purchased a computer for $2,000. The depreciation rate for this type of computer is 20% per year. Determine the worth of the computer after three and a half years.

8. Find the slopes of the following straight lines:

   a. $7x - 2y = 14$ b. $x - 3y = 9$ c. $9x + 2y = 18$

   d. $-2x + y = -4$ e. $x = 5$ f. $y = -3$

   g. $2x - 3 = 4$ h. $x = 5y$ i. $6 - 3y = 1$

9. Find the equation of the straight line containing the given points:

   a. $(-1, 4)$ and $(0, 2)$ b. $(7, 5)$ and $(9, -3)$

   c. $(5, -1)$ and $(1, 11)$ d. $(3, 0)$ and $(3, -6)$

   e. $(4, 5)$ and $(2, 5)$ f. $(6, 1)$ and $(8, -6)$

10. A certain candy company wanted to introduce their new chocolate candy bar. To stimulate sales, the company gave free samples to chosen retail stores. The company collected the data given in TABLE A. Plot the points in Table A to verify that the relationship between the number of subsequent purchases P and the number of free samples distributed S is a straight line, and then determine the equation of that line.

TABLE A

Number of free samples distributed (S)	Number of subsequent purchases (P)
1000	2006
1250	2233
1500	2459
1750	2685
2000	2911
3000	3816
4000	4721

11. FIGURE 2 shows the cumulative weekly sales receipts of a family restaurant over the past year.

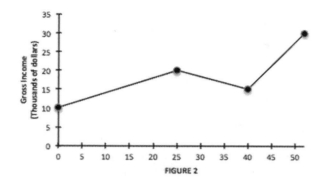

FIGURE 2

    a. Determine the equation relating gross income, I, to time, t, for the first 25-weeks period.
    b. Determine the equation relating I to t for the next 15-weeks period.
    c. Determine the equation relating I to t for the last 12 weeks of the year.

12. A publisher of a current solution manual to a textbook determines that the manufacturing costs directly attributed to each manual are $4 and that the fixed costs are $15,000. The publisher sells each manual for $29.99 per copy.

    a. Determine the equation relating the total cost to the number of manual published.
    b. Determine the equation relating the sales revenue to the number of manual published.
    c. What will the profit be if 2000 manual are published?
    d. Algebraically determine the break-even point for this process.

13. Determine the break-even point in Problem 13 graphically. Which method do you prefer?

14. A manufacturer of calculators determines that the variable costs directly attributable to each calculator are $25 and that the fixed costs are $20,000. Each calculator sells for $99.

    a. Determine the break-even point for this process both graphically and algebraically.
    b. Determine the total cost of the process at the break-even point.
    c. Determine the total sales revenue of the process at the break-even point.
    d. Determine the profit at the break-even point.

15. A manufacturer of cellphone holders has determined that the firm has a break-even point of 3,000 units. Determine the selling price of each holder if each item costs $.50 to manufacture and the process involves fixed cost of $18,000.

16. The supply equation for a commodity is given by $S = x^2 + 300$, and the demand equation is given by $D = -20x + 4000$. Determine the break-even point(s).

17. Determine which of the following equations are quadratic as defined by Equation 2.18, and for those that are quadratic, specify the quadratic variable.

   a. $y = x^2 + 2x$ b. $x = y^2$ c. $x^2 - 6x + 9 = y$

   d. $x - 2y = 4$ e. $p^2 = 5 - D$ f. $y = 2x^3$

   g. $y = \sqrt[3]{x}$ h. $P = -3M^2$ i. $y - 7x^2 = 1$

89. Graph the following quadratic curves by plotting a sufficient number of points to determine the curve' correct shape.

   a. $y = x^2 + 1$ b. $y = 1 - x^2$ c. $y = x^2 - 3x + 2$

   d. $D = -x^2 + x + 2$ e. $R = 3x^2 - 5$ f. $d = 4 - 2x^2$

19. Use the quadratic formula to find the values of x that satisfy the following equations.

   a. $x^2 - x - 2 = 0$ b. $x^2 - 4 = 0$ c. $3x^2 - 12x = 0$

   d. $9x^2 - 5 = 0$ e. $x^2 + 2x = 7$ f. $\frac{1}{4}x^2 - x - 1 = 0$

   g. $2x^2 - 10x + 12 = 0$

20. A small company that manufactures reusable 12-ounces plastic cups monthly profit (in million of dollars) is given by $P(x) = -x^2 + 30x - 60$, where x is the number of 12-ounces cup sold (in millions) per month.

   a. Determine the largest number of cups the company sell and still make a profit?

   b. If the company sell more than the number of cups in part (a), explain how it is possible for it to loose money.

   c. Determine the number of cups the company should sale to maximize the profit, and then find the maximum profit.

21. A charter bus charges $120 per person, plus an additional $5 per person for each unsold seat on the bus. The bus can seat 56 passengers. Let x represent the number of unsold seats.

   a. Determine the total revenue equation relating the revenue, denoted by R, to the number of unsold seats, denoted by x.

   b. Determine the number of unsold seats that will maximize the revenue.

   c. Determine the maximum revenue.

22. A retail store has 40 high-end computers that it must sell within a month. From their record, it is known that the demand, d, per month is related to the price p (in thousands of dollars) by the equation $d = 320 - 2.5p^2$. Determine the maximum price that will result in no inventory at the end of the month.

23. Determine which of the following equations represent polynomial curves and, or those that do, give the degree:

   a. $y = 3x^2 - 5x$

   b. $y^2 = 1 - 7x^2 + 2x^3$

   c. $y = -x^4 + 7x^3 + 2x - 1$

   d. $y = \sqrt[3]{x} + 1$

   e. $y^{1/2} = x - 3$

   f. $y - 7x^3 = 1$

   g. $y^4 = 7$

   h. $9x^7 - 4x + 1 = y$

24. The revenue for a retail company (in millions of dollars) is given by $R = 1.5x^3 - 27x^2 + 162x - 74$, where x = 0 corresponds to the year 2000.

   a. Determine the revenue for $x = 0$, $x = 8$, and $x = 15$.
   b. Graph the equation.
   c. Is revenue always increasing? Explain.

25. The yearly costs (in millions of dollars) for a company is approximated by the equation:

   $C = 2.3x^2 - 36.8x + 30$, where x is the number of years.

   a. Determine the costs for x = 0, x = 3, and x = 12.
   b. Graph the equation.
   c. Determine the number of years that will minimize costs?

26. Determine which of the following equations are exponential equations, as determined by Definition 2.15, and for those that are, the values of a and b.

   a. $y = 3(2^x)$

   b. $y = (5^x)2$

   c. $y = (-9)^x$

   d. $y = (6^x)^3$

   e. $y = 7(3^{-x})$

   f. $y = 4(2^{x^3})$

   g. $y = 8^{x+1}$

   h. $y = \sqrt{2}(-2)^x$

   i. $y = \left(\frac{1}{5}\right)^{2x}$

27. The number of remaining bacteria that in a certain culture that is subjected to refrigeration can be approximated by the equation:

   $Remaining\ Bacteria = (Original\ Number\ of\ Bacteria)e^{-0.048t}$

   where t is the time, in hours, that the culture has been refrigerated, and e known as "Oiler's number," is the irrational number 2.8128.... Using this equation determine the number of remaining bacteria in this culture for:

   a. an original of bacteria of 200,000 that is refrigerated for 15 hours.
   b. an original of bacteria of 200,000 that is refrigerated for 24 hours.
   c. an original of bacteria of 300,000 that is refrigerated for 48 hours.
   d. an original of bacteria of 400,000 that is refrigerated for 72 hours.

28. Rachel is a chemistry professor at a world renown university who has just discovered a new radioactive element. The number of grams of this radioactive element left after t minutes is given by:

Remaining Amount = (Initial Amount)$e^{-0.03014t}$

Using this formula, determine the amount of radioactive material remaining after:

a. 50 minutes, assuming that the initial amount is 200 grams.
b. 75 minutes, assuming that the initial amount is 350 grams

CHAPTER 3

1. For $3000 being deposited in an account for 4 years that yields 5% annual interest compounded semiannually.

   a. Determine the values of i, n, and $P(o)$ that would be used to determine the amount in the account at the end of the fourth year.
   b. Determine the balance in the account at the end of the fourth year.

2. Mr. Jones invested $5,000 from a co-worker who charges 3.75% interest compound annually. Determine his debt after 2 years.

3. Marie deposits $1,500 into an account that pays 4.25% interest compounded quarterly. How much will she have after 3 years?

4. Determine the balance after 2 years resulting from $2,500 being deposited in a savings account that yields 2.75% interest compounded monthly.

5. Some institutions use an *approximate year* rather than a calendar year for certain interest computations. In this method, every month is assumed to have exactly 30 days, resulting in an approximate year of 360 days. Using an approximate year, set-up and determine the balance after 2 years for an initial deposit of $3,500 if the interest rate is 2.89% compounded daily.

6. Determine the future value of $10,000 after 5 years if it is deposited in an account that pays 4.25%

   a. annually
   b. semi-annually
   c. quarterly
   d. daily(assume each year has 360 days)

7. A student at Fairleigh Dickinson University has $3,000 to deposit. Should she put it in a bank offering 3% interest compounded quarterly or one offering 4.25% interest compounded annually?

8. Determine the present value of $20,000 due in in 6 years at

   a. 3% interest compounded annually.
   b. 5% interest compounded annually.
   c. 9% interest compounded annually.
   d. Based on the present values determined in parts a – c, what can you say is the relationship between present values and the interest rate?

9. Michael is going to college in 4 years and decides to place the sum of money in an account which yields 3.75% compounded quarterly. If he needs $100,000 in 4 years, determine the amount of deposit.

10. Mr. Smith has two buyers for his car. Buyer A will pay $15,000 immediately and another $30,000 in 3 years. Buyer B will pay $9,000 immediately and another $35,000 in 2 years. Which is the better offer if the interest rates are 3% compounded annually?

11. Given $i = \left(\dfrac{FV}{PV}\right)^{1/n} - 1$. Use this formula to determine the annual interest rate required to convert $20,000 to $25,000 in 8 years.

12. Given $i = \left(\dfrac{FV}{PV}\right)^{1/n} - 1$. Use this formula to determine the annual interest rate required to double an investment after 12 years.

13. Carolyn's friend invited her to invest $5,000 in a venture that will return $800 in 1 year, another $1,500 in 2 years, and a final investment $3,500 in 3 years. Determine whether or not this is profitable investment if the current rates are 2.75% per annum compounded annually.

14. Determine the present value of an opportunity that will return $600 in half a year, $1,200 in a year and three quarter, and $1,900 in three years if the current interest rate is 3% per annum compounded quarterly.

15. A person can invest $60,000 now and receive $15,000 at the end of each quarter for the next 2 years plus an additional $10,000 at the end of the second year, or he can invest $80,000 now and receive $25,000 at the end of the quarter for the next 2 years. Which opportunity is the better investment at 3% interest per annum compounded quarterly?

16. Determine the present of a $100 return every month for the next 8 years at 5% annual interest compounded monthly.

17. Determine the present value of an investment that will return $700 at the end of each year for the next 4 years at annual interest rate of 3.75%.

18. Mr. Bates has $5,000 to invest. Determine the NPV of his investment if he lends the money to his neighbor who repays him $800 at the end of each year for the next 4 years. Use an annual interest rate of 4.15%.

19. Mrs. Newman can invest $100,000 now and receive $2,500 at the end of each quarter for the next 3 years plus an additional $40,000 at the end of the second year, or she can invest the $100,000 now and receive $4,500 at the end of each quarter for the next 3 years. Which opportunity is more profitable at 3.75% annual interest per annum compounded quarterly.

20. A bond pays $75 every month. How much should you pay for the bond (present value), if you want a 4.25% return on your money and the bond has a 12 payments left. Additionally, on the twelfth payment you will also receive $1,000, which is the original price of the bond.

21. Determine the future value of an ordinary annuity in which $2,000 is deposited at the end of every six months for 5 years at 3% annual interest compounded annually.

22. Jenny deposits $30 at the end of each week in an account at 4.5% annual interest compounded weekly. How much money will she have to spend on presents for her nieces and nephews when she takes the money out at the end of 40 weeks?

23. To provide for their only child's education, the Rogers deposit $2,000 every six months(June 30 – December 31) for 17 years. Determine the value of the annuity just after their last payment, which occurs on December 31, if their investment plan pays 5% annual interest compounded semiannually.

24. Determine the monthly payment for a 25 year, $40,000 mortgage, having a 7.5% interest rate.

25. Determine the total interest paid for the mortgage in Problem 24.

26. Mr. Richards decides to sell his Lamborghini to his friend. The mortgage obtained by his friend for this car is for $150,000 over 3 years at 4.25%.

    a.   Determine the monthly installment.
    b.   Determine the total interest paid for this mortgage.
    c.   Complete the first three lines of an amortization schedule for this mortgage.

27. Andy McDonald borrows $8,000 from a bank for a new car loan at 7% interest add-on. Determine the monthly installment and the total interest paid if the loan is to be repaid over 3 years.

28. The Parkers have decided to apply for a one year, $7,000, vacation loan, that is calculated using the add-on method with 5.5% interest rate.

    a.   Determine the total interest paid for this loan.
    b.   Determine the monthly payment for this loan.

29. a. Determine the monthly payment for a $12,000, 6 year, discounted loan at 4%.
    b. Determine the cash received when this loan is granted.

30. Gina needs $25,000 for her college tuition. She takes out a 6 year, discounted loan at 3.75% interest rate.

    a.   Determine how much she borrow to realize $25,000 after the loan is granted.
    b.   Determine the monthly payment for the loan amount determined in part (a).
    c.   Determine the total interest charge for the loan amount determined in part (a).

31. Determine the present value of an annuity due in which $50 is deposited at the beginning of each quarter for 10 years at 2.75% compounded quarterly.

32. Determine the present value of an annuity due in which $200 is deposited on January 1st and July 1st for 15 years at 3.25% annual interest rate.

33. Determine the future value of an annuity due in which $75 is deposited at the beginning of each week for 2 years at 4% annual interest compounded weekly.

34. Ms. Carter deposits $1,000 at the beginning of each month in an account at 4.25% annual interest compounded monthly. How much money will she have to spend on a new car when she takes the money out at the end of 15 months?

35. Determine the total value after 3 years of an annuity due of $10 per day at 5.5% annual interest compounded daily.

36. For problems a – f, find the effective interest rate for the stated rates.

   a. 3% compounded annually.
   b. 2% compounded semi-annually.
   c. 4% compounded quarterly.
   d. 5% compounded monthly.
   e. 6% compounded daily.
   f. 7% compounded continuously.

CHAPTER 4

For 1 – 11, determine whether or not the given relationships are functions.

1.

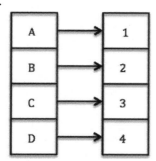

2.

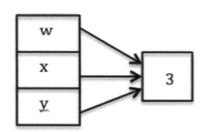

3.

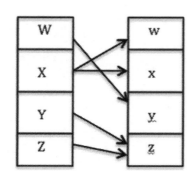

4.

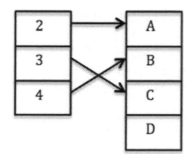

5.

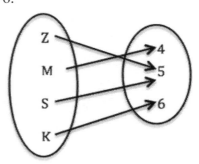

6.

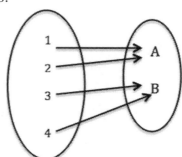

7.

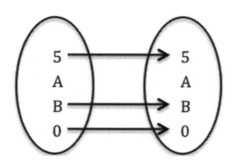

8.

9.

x	0	1	2	3
y	5	6	7	8

10.

x	2	4	6	8
y	1	3	1	3

11.

x	1	3	1	7
y	4	0	9	7

12. Determine whether or not the following assignments constitute a function.

    a. The assignment between students in a class and their seats.
    b. The assignment between driver license plates to their cars.
    c. The assignment between social security numbers to their owners.
    d. The assignment between student identification numbers to student names.

13. Consider the function $S(x) = x^2 - 60x + 900$, $0 \le x \le 30$, x is an integer.

    a. What is the domain of the function? (List the values.)
    b. What is the range of the function?
    c. What values of the range are actually taken by S? (List them.)

For 14 – 23, the following equations relate values of x to values of y. For each equation list a possible domain and range to qualify the sets of numbers and the equation as a function.

14. $y = 2x + 7$

15. $y = \dfrac{4}{x+1}$

16. $y = \sqrt{x} + 1$

17. $y = -x^2 + 10$

18. $y = x^2 - \dfrac{2}{x}$

19. $f(x) = \dfrac{x-1}{x+2}$

20. $f(x) = x^2 - 6x + 10$

21. $f(x) = \dfrac{3-x^2}{x+7}$

22. $y = \dfrac{x+3}{(x-1)(x+4)}$

23. $f(x) = |x - 3| + 1$

24. Determine whether or not the relationship defined by $y = 4 - 7x$, $0 \le x < \infty$, is a function. Determine whether the inverse relationship is a function. (*Hint*: Solve for x in terms of y.)

25. Determine whether or not the relationship $y = \sqrt[4]{x}$ is a function for $0 \le x < \infty$.

26. Determine whether or not the relationship $y = \pm\sqrt[4]{x}$ is a function for $0 \le x < \infty$.

27. Determine whether or not $C = p^2 + 16$, $0 \leq p \leq 6$, is a function. Is the inverse relationship a function for $16 \leq C \leq 52$? (*Hint*: Solve for p in terms of C.)

For 28 – 39, given the function $f(x) = x^2 - 3x - 10$, find

28. $f(0)$ 29. $f(-2)$ 30. $f(3)$ 31. $f(5a)$

32. $f(7\Delta x)$ 33. $f(a - b)$ 34. $f(x - \Delta x)$ 35. $f(x + h)$

36. $f\left(\frac{2}{x}\right)$ 37. $f(\sqrt{x})$ 38. $f(-4m)$ 39. $f(a + 2b)$

40. An owner of a retail store determined that the supply for a particular brand of cellphone is related to cost by the function $S(c) = c^2 - 38c + 361$. Determine the domain for this function so that the resulting function represents a plausible supply curve.

For 41 – 44, find the average rate of change in the function $f(x) = x^2 + 5x + 6$ over the following intervals:

41. $[2, 7]$ 42. $[-1, 4]$ 43. $[0, 5]$ 44. $[-4, -2]$

For 45 – 50, determine the average rate of change in the following functions over the interval $[-1, 3]$.

45. $f(x) = 2x + 7$ 46. $g(x) = -x^2 + 3x - 2$ 47. $p(c) = c^2 + 4$

48. $y(x) = 1 - 3x^2$ 49. $h(t) = t^2 - 9x + 14$ 50. $d(z) = 1 - 9z$

51. Use Equation 4.5 to find the general expression for the average rate of change in the function $f(x) = x^2 - 9x$ over the interval $[x_1, x_2]$. Use this expression to find the average rates of change over the intervals given in Problem 11.

52. a. Sketch the function $f(x) = x^2 - 2x + 3$ and graphically determine the slope of the tangent lines at the point (2, 3).

    b. Complete TABLE 1. Do the values in the last column approach the slope determined in part a. ?

TABLE 1

x_1	x_2	y_1	y_2	Average rate $= \dfrac{y_2 - y_1}{x_2 - x_1}$
2	3.5	3		
2	2.7	3		
2	2.1	3		
2	2.05	3		

For 53 – 60, use Equation 4.8 to find a general expression for the instantaneous rate of change in the given function. Use this result to find the instantaneous rate of change at $x = 2$ and $x = -3$.

53. $f(x) = 7x + 4$

54. $f(x) = x^2 - 7x + 10$

55. $f(x) = 2x^3$

56. $f(x) = 1 - 2x$

56. $f(x) = \dfrac{x}{x-3}$

57. $f(x) = x - \dfrac{4}{x}$

58. $f(x) = \dfrac{1}{x^3}$

59. $f(x) = x^3 - 4x^2 + 7x - 1$

60. $f(x) = \dfrac{1}{5}x^2 + 3$

61. Consider the function

$$f(x) = \begin{cases} x+1, & x \le 2 \\ -x+5, & x > 2 \end{cases}$$

which is sketched in Figure 1.

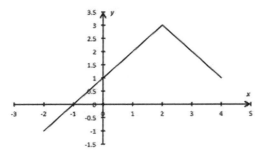

Figure 1

   a. Determine graphically whether this curve has a tangent at $x = 2$.

   b. Compute the average rates of change for this function over the intervals having $x = 2$ as one end point and the second end point given successively by 2.3, 1.99, 2.05, 1.95, 2.15, 1.97, 1.98, 2.13, 2.003, and 1.999. Do these rates approach a fixed value? What can you conclude about the instantaneous rate of change at $x = 2$?

62. A retail company's sales are known to be related to advertising expenditures by the function $S(x) = -75x^2 + 9{,}000x + 225{,}000$, where x denotes the monthly advertising expenditures in thousands of dollar.

   a. Find the instantaneous rate of change in the sales with respect to advertising expenditures.

   b. Using your answer in part a, determine whether an increase in advertising would increase sales if the present advertising budget is $50,000. Would the situation be different with a $60,000 advertising budget?

63. A certain company's total sales, in millions of dollars, are given by the function $R(x) = \frac{2}{3}x^2 + 4x$, where x denotes the number of years the company has been in operation.

   a. Determine the company's average growth rate in sales for its first 5 years in business.

   b. Determine the company's instantaneous rate of growth after its fifth year in business.

   c. What will the company's total sales be at the end of the eighth year if sales continue to follow the given function?

   d. What will the company's total sales be at the end of the eighth year if the growth in sales after the fifth year always equals the growth achieved at the end of the fifth year?

For 64 – 71, find $f'(x)$.

64. $f(x) = x^4 - 2x^3 + 7x - 6$

65. $f(x) = -3x^2 + 8x$

66. $f(x) = (x^2 + 6)x^7$

67. $f(x) = (2x + 5)(x^2 - 3)$

68. $f(x) = e^x + 2x - 10$

69. $f(x) = \frac{x^2}{3} - \frac{1}{2}e^x + \frac{5x}{4}$

70. $f(x) = \frac{6x^3 - 3x^2 + 14x - 7}{2x - 1}$

71. $f(x) = \frac{9}{2}x^2 - \frac{1}{3}x$

For 72 – 77, find $\frac{dy}{dx}$.

72. $y = x^2 - 5x - 7$

73. $y = 7x^3 + x^2 - 4x + 1$

74. $y = \frac{x^5}{3} - 2x + 7e^x$

75. $y = (2x - 3)(x + 1)$

76. $y = \frac{x^3 - 3x^2 + 5x - 15}{x - 3}$

77. $y = \frac{4}{3}x - 12e^x + 15.2$

78. From past experience it is known that an increase in gas price leads to a decrease in the demand for SUVs. Based on this information, determine which of the following equations may possibly relate the demand D for SUVs to the gas price p.

   a. $D = 100p^2 + 3p + 500$

   b. $D = \frac{500}{p^2}$

   c. $D = 3,000 - 5p^3$

   d. $D = p^3 + 900$

79. Determine the values of x for the function illustrated in Figure 2 between or at which

   a. the derivative is positive,
   b. the derivative is negative, and
   c. the derivative is zero.

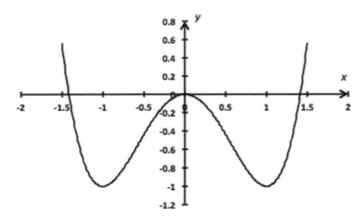

Figure 2

For 80 – 93, find $f'(x)$.

80. $f(x) = (x^3 + 2)e^{8x}$

81. $f(x) = (x^3 + 9x^2 - 10x)(3x^2 + 7x)$

82. $f(x) = \dfrac{x^4 - 3x}{e^{5x}}$

83. $f(x) = \left(x^{1/3} + x^{-2/3}\right)(x^{-7} + x^2)$

84. $f(x) = \dfrac{e^{-9x} + 7}{x^2 - 6}$

85. $f(x) = (7 - 4x)^3$

86. $f(x) = (x^2 + 3e^{-5x})^8$

87. $f(x) = \sqrt{2x + 5}$

88. $f(x) = \sqrt[3]{(e^{2x} - 4)^2}$

89. $f(x) = \dfrac{2}{x^3} - \dfrac{7}{x^4}$

90. $f(x) = x^{-10} + x^{-1/4} - x^{-7}$

91. $f(x) = \dfrac{1}{(1 - e^{5x})^2}$

92. $f(x) = \dfrac{(1 - 3x)^5}{(x^3 - x^6)}$

93. $f(x) = \dfrac{(2x + 7)^5}{(2x + 7)^{-3}}$

For 94 – 96, find $\dfrac{DS}{Dx}$ using the chain rule.

94. $S = E^2 - 5E + 1, \quad E = 2x + 7.$

95. $S = 5 - E^3, \quad E = 5x^2 - 3x + 9.$

96. $S = \dfrac{E + 1}{E - 3}, \quad E = 1 - 4x - x^2.$

For 97 – 102, find $\dfrac{dy}{dx}$ and $\dfrac{d^2y}{dx^2}$ and evaluate the second derivative at the point $x = -1$ and $x = 1$.

97. $y = 7x^4 - 3x^2 + 6x - 1$ 98. $y = 3x - 2$

99. $y = 5 - x^2$ 100. $y = e^{12x}$

101. $y = 10x^2 e^{8x}$ 102. $y = e^x + 2x$

103. Figure C represents the distance traveled as a function of time for Mrs. McDonald's 4.95-mile trip to a grocery store. The equation illustrated in Figure 3 is $D = -0.25t^3 + 1.25t^2 + 0.15t$, where D is the distance traveled in miles, and t is measured in minutes from the start of the trip.

    a. Determine the general expression for the speed of Mrs. McDonald's car at any time during the trip.
    b. Determine the speed that would be indicated by Mrs. McDonald's speedometer at $t = 1$ minutes.
    c. Determine a general expression for Mrs. McDonald's acceleration at any time during the trip. $\left(Hint: Acceleration = \dfrac{d(speed)}{dt} = \dfrac{d^2D}{dt^2} = D''(t).\right)$

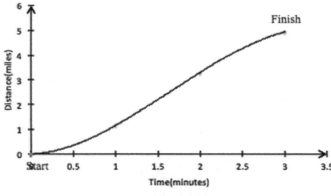

Figure 3

    d. Using your answer in part c., determine Mrs. McDonald's acceleration at $t = 1$ minute and $t = 3$ minutes. What is the significance of the negative sign at $t = 3$ minutes?

CHAPTER 5

In Exercises 1 – 5, find the maximum and minimum values of the given functions two ways: First, graph the functions, visually locating the optimal points and, second, use differentiation.

1. $y = 4x^2 - 16x + 5,$ $\qquad$ $(0 \leq x \leq 4)$

2. $y = -x^2 + 14x + 2.5,$ $\qquad$ $(3 \leq x \leq 10)$

3. $y = 2.5x^2 - 5x + 7,$ $\qquad$ $(0 \leq x \leq 5)$

4. $y = -2x + 4,$ $\qquad$ $(15 \leq x \leq 35)$

5. $y = -6x^2 + 108x,$ $\qquad$ $(0 \leq x \leq 9)$

In Exercises 6 – 12, use the first derivative to determine maximum and minimum values of the given functions.

6. $D(t) = 2t^3 - 24t + 5,$ $\qquad$ $(-4 \leq t \leq 3)$

7. $P(x) = x^3 - 27x - 2,$ $\qquad$ $(-2 \leq x \leq 5)$

8. $R(n) = 4n^3 - 48n - 1,$ $\qquad$ $(-3 \leq n \leq 4)$

9. $y(x) = x^3 - 75x + 17,$ $\qquad$ $(-6 \leq x \leq 5)$

10. $T(c) = c^3 + 6c^2 + 9c - 7,$ $\qquad$ $(-4 \leq c \leq 3)$

11. $x(t) = \frac{2}{3}t^3 + \frac{1}{2}t^2 - 3t + 25,$ $\quad$ $(-1 \leq t \leq 2)$

12. $y(x) = (x - 20)(x - 30),$ $\qquad$ $(10 \leq x \leq 35)$

13. A computer manufacturer has found that the profit P (in dollars) obtained from selling x computers per week is given by the function $P(x) = -x^2 + 500x - 8,500.$

   a. Determine how many computers the manufacturer should produce to maximize profits.

   b. What is the maximum profit that can be realized?

14. The manufacturer described in Problem 13 also has determined that the total cost of producing x items, denoted by TC (in dollars) is given by

   $$TC = \frac{x^2}{4000} - 14x + 20,000.$$

   a. Determine the number of items that should be produced if the manufacturer's goal is to minimize total cost rather than to maximize profit.

   b. What is the minimum total cost? Is the answer reasonable?

15. A small company found that the total cost TC (in dollars) of producing x items is given by the equation $TC = \frac{2}{3} x^3 - 20x^2 - 1,600x + 24,000.$

   a. Determine the number of units this company should produce to minimize its production cost.

b. Assume that the company can sell all units that it produces a fixed price of \$415 per unit. Determine how many units this company should produce to maximize its profit.

16. Find the maximum and minimum values of the function given by

$$y = \begin{cases} -x^2 - 4x + 6, & (0 \le x \le 3) \\ x + 2, & (3 < x \le 5) \end{cases}$$

17. Find the maximum and minimum values of the function given by

$$y = \begin{cases} -x^2 - 6x + 5, & (0 \le x \le 2) \\ x + 2, & (2 < x \le 5) \end{cases}$$

18. A computer manufacturer can sell all units produced at \$290 per unit. The total cost C (in dollars) in producing x units per week is given by $C = 10,000 + 40x + \frac{1}{2}x^2$.

   a. Determine an expression (model) for profit as a function of x.

   b. Determine an appropriate domain for x if the weekly production capacity is limited to 300 units?

   c. Determine the maximum weekly profit.

19. A dishwasher manufacturer can sell all the dishwashers it can produce. The total cost for producing x dishwashers per week is given by the equation $C = 400x + 3,000$. The unit price, p, is related to the number of dishwashers sold by the equation $p = 800 - 4x$.

   a. Determine an equation for the revenue equation.

   b. Determine an equation for the profit.

   c. Determine an appropriate domain if the production capacity is 80 units per week.

   d. How many units should be produced in a week to maximize profit?

20. Redo Problem 19 if the production capacity is only 30 dishwashers per week?

21. Determine the marginal revenue if

   a. $R(x) = 35x$

   b. $R(x) = 300x - \frac{1}{2}x^2$

   c. $R(x) = 3.25 - 0.000055x^2$

22. Determine the marginal revenue found in Problem 21 for both $x = 20,000$ and $x = 60,000$.

23. Determine the marginal cost if

 a. $C(x) = \frac{x^2}{2,000} + 7x + 10,000$

 b. $C(x) = 90x + 1,500$

 c. $C(x) = 0.52x + 20,000$

24. The cost of placing an order is $5.25, and the cost of storing one item per year is $20.

 a. Determine the optimal order size (EOQ) if 1000 items are required during a year.

 b. Determine the number of orders that will be placed during a year.

 c. Determine the total reorder costs over the course of a year.

 d. Determine the total storage costs over the course of a year.

25. Assume that **Figure 1** adequately describes the inventory situation of a small computer dealer.

 a. Determine the economic order quantity (EOQ) for the dealer.

 b. Find the total number of orders placed during a year.

 c. Determine the total number of computers sold during a year.

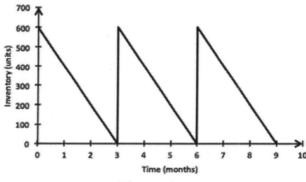

Figure 1

26. Determine the reorder point and cycle time for Problem 24, assuming the lead time is 4 days.

27. Determine the increase in the total national income of a society modeled by Equation 5.12 and Equation 5.14 if $m = 0.5$ and business investment is increased by $12 million.

28. Determine the decrease in the total national income of a society modeled by Equation 5.12 and 5.14 if $m = 0.75$ and business investment is decreased by $8 millions.

29. Redo Problem 27 for a society modeled by Equations 5.12 and 5.13.

CHAPTER 6

1. Find the average-value, straight-line fit for the data given in TABLE 1.

TABLE 1

Price ($)	1	2	3	4	5	6	7	8	9	10
Demand ($100)	10	11	12	9	9	8	10	11	10	9

2. The profits for a small computer company are given in TABLE 2 for a 7-year period.

TABLE 2

Year	2003	2004	2005	2006	2007	2008	2009
Profit ($1000)	150	130	175	145	139	165	147

  a. Find the average-value, straight-line fit for the given data.

  b. Compute consecutive 3-year moving averages for the given data.

3. A medium used car dealership is considering an increase in it advertising budget to increase sales. As the manager of the establishment, you are asked to advise the owner whether to increase its advertisement budget. The information you collected is shown in **TABLE 3**.

TABLE 3

Year	2010	2011	2012	2013	2014	2015	2016
Advertising ($1000)	140	160	150	160	160	150	160
Sales ($1000)	40	45	47	43	41	47	42

  a. What will be your observation based on the data?

  b. Determine the least-squares straight line for the data.

  c. Based on the line found in Part b, would you advise the owner that it is worthwhile to increase the advertising budget?

4. Consider the data given in **TABLE 4.**

TABLE 4

x	0	1	2	3	4	5	6	7	8	9	10
y	5	7	6	9	8	5	10	5	12	11	10

  a. Plot the data points, either by hand or using an Excel scatter diagram, and determine whether a straight-line approximation for the trend line seems reasonable.
  b. Determine the least-squares straight line for the data, either by hand or using Excel.
  c. Calculate the least-squares error for this line.
  d. Draw any other straight line that appears to fit the data reasonably well and compare the least-squares error of this line to the result from Part c.

5. The number of window air conditioners sold each year by a retail store are given in TABLE 5.

TABLE 5

Year	2010	2011	2012	2013	2014	2015	2016
Units Sold	30	17	25	20	19	22	23

    a. Plot the data points, either by hand or using Excel

    b. Determine the least-squares straight line for the data, either by hand or using Excel.

    c. Use the line found in Part b to project the number of units sold in 2017.

6. Using Excel, find the least-squares quadratic trend line for the data listed in TABLE 6.

TABLE 6

x	0	1	2	3	4
y	10	6	7	8	12

7. Complete **TABLE 7** for the data given in **TABLE 6** and show that the least-squares error is 237.9224. Here y_c denotes the y-value obtained from evaluating the least-squares quadratic curve, $y = 1.1429x^2 - 3.9714x + 9.6857$, at the appropriate values of x.

TABLE 7

x_i	y_i	y_c	$e(x_i)$	$[e(x_i)]^2$
0	10			
1	6			
2	7			
3	8			
4	12			
Sums:				

8. Find the least-squares straight line for the data in **TABLE 6** and then calculate the lease-squares error for this line.

    a. How does this error compared with the error found in Problem 7?

    b. Draw both the least-squares quadratic curve and the least-squares straight line on the same graph and compare visually.

9. Consider the three data points $(-2, 24)$, $(0, -8)$, and $(4, 0)$.

    a. Using Equations 6.6 through 6.8, determine the three simultaneous equations required to fit a least-squares quadratic curve to these data.

    b. Verify that the solutions to the equations found in Part a are $a = 3, b = -10$, and $c = -8$.

10. Using Excel, find the least-squares quadratic trend line for the data listed in TABLE 8.

TABLE 8

x	−3	− 2	− 1	0	1	2	3
y	20	15	12	13	17	23	30

11. Using a spread sheet program, find the least-squares exponential trend line for the data listed in **TABLE 9**.

TABLE 9

x	0	1	2	3	4
y	25	60	150	200	500

12. The profits of a new rapidly growing company for its first 6 years are given in **TABLE 10**.

TABLE 10

Year	2000	2001	2002	2003	2004	2005
Profit (millions)	10	25	39	47	100	150

    a. Using a spread sheet program, find the least-squares exponential trend line for this data.

    b. Use the trend equation found in Part a to project profit for 2008.

21316263R00074

Made in the USA
Columbia, SC
17 July 2018